NEW COLLECTED POEMS

New Collected Poems

STEPHEN SPENDER

edited by Michael Brett

faber and faber

First published in 2004
by Faber & Faber Limited
Bloomsbury House
74–77 Great Russell Street,
London WC1B 3DA
Published in the United States by Faber and Faber Inc.,
an affiliate of Farrar, Straus and Giroux LLC, New York
This paperback edition first published in 2018

Photoset by RefineCatch Limited, Bungay, Suffolk
Printed in England by Martins the Printers, Berwick-upon-Tweed

A CIP record for this book
is available from the British Library

ISBN 978-0-571-34772-8

Contents

1939

RUINS AND VISIONS (1942)

Part One: A Separation

Part Two: Ironies of War

Part Three: Deaths

THE EDGE OF BEING (1949)

1949–1970

Introduction

Stephen Spender described himself as 'an autobiographer in search of a form'. The interplay between his personal life and the public history of the twentieth century provides the thematic basis for his prose autobiography, *World Within World* (1951), and the poetry of the first half of his career. Spender's early work is marked by the exigencies of history within which it was written, and an awareness of this is vital to its understanding. As the poetry ceased to be influenced by those momentous events which had guided Europe into the Second World War, it became less involved in social themes, turning more resolutely towards the lyrical self. The narrative of his life – the public world and the private – directly informs the themes and styles of the seven Faber and Faber volumes, which are collected here for the first time, in the form in which they originally appeared.

Spender prepared two editions of *Collected Poems*, published in 1955 and 1985. On both occasions he availed himself of the opportunity to reorganise his work into thematic and chronological sequences, and to revise in accordance with his current thoughts on metre, diction, and clarity of expression. He insisted that he never lost sight of the original inspiration for a poem, and that subsequent revisions were an attempt to find greater accuracy, a closer verbal correlative for the idea of the poem. Though he professed to work from the same 'memory of the circumstances from which the poem arose', his revisionism produced new versions which share a title and an inspiration perhaps, yet which are quite distinct from their precursors. In some cases, he revised poems after an interval of more than fifty years. For example, 'In 1929', one of Spender's earliest compositions, is a memorial to a walking tour in Germany. The poem is deeply personal and historically portentous, yet Spender's revisions transform the poem into a meditation upon what has happened in European history, rather than upon what his younger self apprehended. Moreover, Spender was so censorious an editor of his own work that many poems did not survive into *Collected Poems 1928–1985*, which is replaced by the present edition.

An alternative edition of Spender's verse would incorporate the various revisions of his oeuvre, charting the development of the early work from its first appearance, through its 1955 revision, to its final version in 1985, which was essentially a re-visioning of his autobiography in verse. But for the purposes of this first posthumous edition I have chosen to uphold the claims of publishing history to present Spender's verse career as it played out in publication. It is possible to trace a clear development through a variety of modes and philosophical positions which the later revisions obscure. The 1930s work underwent the most extensive revision, and in the early part of this book we see the poetry of a politicised man in the 1930s, rather than that work as it was transformed by his mature self in the 1950s and again in the 1980s. Readers who wish to examine Spender's different approaches to his own oeuvre should therefore refer to the two previous editions of the *Collected Poems*.

Much has been written about the young 'Thirties Poets'. Spender, W. H. Auden, Louis MacNeice, Cecil Day Lewis and others were part of a generation of individualists who shared aesthetic and political tendencies which have become synonymous with 1930s literature – most significantly an enthusiasm for socialist thought and a fascination with industrial modernity. They came to attention in the Hogarth Press anthologies *New Signatures* (1932) and *New Country* (1933), where they challenged the Georgians' vision of a Little England. Spender, like his peers, revered the work of modernist T. S. Eliot, and the sober moral imperative of the poets of the First World War; but the lyrical exhortations in his early volumes owe as much to German poets such as Friedrich Hölderlin and Ernst Toller as they do to the traditions of British verse. Spender was already on his own creative trajectory when he became known as one of the 'Auden Group', and his reluctance to alter his work in the light of his friend's criticism (Auden's impatience with what he saw as Spender's incorrigible Romanticism) suggests a relationship of aesthetic independence.

The disparity between these two Oxford poets' sensibilities led T. S. Eliot, poetry editor at Faber and Faber, to assert as much in the blurb for Spender's *Poems* (1933): 'If Auden is the satirist of this poetical renaissance, Spender is its lyric poet.' It is a sweeping analysis of their work (one which Spender feared would cause Auden offence) but it identifies an important difference between early Auden's thoughtful austerity and early Spender's exuberant emotionalism. It is this exuberance – occasionally flowering into socialist exhortations inspired by the Soviet cinema – which Spender, with the perspective of the tumultuous events of the mid-century and after, tended to trim back, or discard, in his revisions.

The assimilation of political language and polemic into verse disturbed yet intrigued the modernist old guard, who maintained strict aestheticism in art and literature. With worldly determination, the young writers took up the socialist cause. They hoped to assist in the struggle against those Fascist ideologies which were gaining ground in continental Europe. Spender absorbed the imagery of European crisis into his lyrics: the emaciated hunger marchers; Van der Lubbe, duped arsonist of the Reichstag. *Vienna*, Spender's only long poem, was composed at a furious rate in the wake of the failed socialist revolt of 1934. It was published quickly in order to seize the historical moment. Spender finally agreed with Eliot's verdict that he had not worked at 'sufficient distance' from the occasion which had provoked the poem, and he accepted Virginia Woolf's assertion that 'artists can only help one if they don't try to', advising him to steer clear of the exigencies of politics. With a longer view of history, we can see that *Vienna* examines the significance of a tragic defeat along the road to war, while it relates public events to a private relationship. Spender reassessed his experiences in 'Returning to Vienna, 1947', which elucidates the themes of the original poem.

The Still Centre (1939) connects the individualised self to the sphere of social action, establishing the tension between these realities as its central motif. The volume brings together the remainder of Spender's 1930s work, including his Spanish poems. Spender had been engaged as a propagandist for the Republican cause during the Civil War, and with John Lehmann he edited *Poems for Spain* (1939), work by English and Spanish writers directly inspired by the conflict. The poets widely regarded the death of García Lorca as a shocking symbol of the new oppression, while General Franco's victory augured the inexorable rise of European Fascism.

In his autobiography, Spender describes himself and his peers as members of the 'Divided Generation', whose early work is yoked to the political climate in which it was created. They had aligned themselves with the cause of peace and social justice, which had failed to materialise, and they were forced instead to seek in verse 'an attitude which would be independent of external events'. In this vein, *Ruins and Visions* (1942) depicts the coalescence of private and public histories; the outbreak of war in 1939 coincided with the break-up of Spender's first marriage. Confessional lyrics of personal tragedy and self-criticism are set against the backdrop of conflict, and the volume moves towards hopeful resolution in the security of Spender's second marriage. *Poems of Dedication* (1947) is preoccupied with the death of Spender's sister-in-law Margaret Spender, and exhibits a further relinquishing of social themes. His verse during this period increasingly pursues philosophical meditations upon mortality and perception, which continue in *The Edge of Being* (1949), a volume heavily marked by his experiences in London during the Blitz and its aftermath. In the later volumes Spender achieves a relaxed, laconic style. *The Generous Days* (1971) and *Dolphins* (1994) emerged at long intervals and the poems are ruminative and often nostalgic. The passing of friends from the 1930s generation inspires a number of valedictions, while Spender's occasional diary poems and childhood reminiscences are among the most poignant in his oeuvre.

Spender's literary career can be divided into two phases which are demarcated by the middle of the century. He apprehended the end of an era after the Second World War, which he described as a 'barrier of violence and devastation' separating individuals from their pre-war selves; the first *Collected Poems* and his autobiography served as a bookend to this era. Spender's poetic output diminished and he became known as an eminent critic, editor and commentator on literature and the arts. His creative attention turned more to the reinterpretation and revision of his earlier work; he did this in the light of criticism, and with an awareness of the insufficiency of his youthful grasp of political reality, when he had endorsed Soviet Russia as an example of benevolent and functioning socialism. For the West, Communism would be the road not taken, but for many young writers of the 1930s, the insidious reality of Stalin's regime was still a well-kept secret. To them, the world-state was a possible, palpable future, and an inspiration.

The poems in this edition are for those readers who wish to see the actual literature of the period; they provide the only accurate depiction of Spender's verse career. *Collected Poems* 1928–1985 was the product of Spender's final ethical and aesthetic intelligence, and the present edition provides a narrative in which that ethical and aesthetic intelligence may be seen in its development.

A Note on the Text

The content of the original volumes has been preserved in all but one instance: two poems, 'Tod und das Maedchen' and 'Wings of the Dove', which appeared in *Ruins and Visions* (1942), were superseded by new versions which fall into a thematic sequence in *Poems of Dedication* (1947). The earlier versions have therefore been omitted.

The dates throughout refer to publication. The supplementary sections are chronological selections of Spender's previously uncollected verse, verse drama and translation. Unfinished or ephemeral pieces have not been included. Spender published widely, and it is possible, and regrettable, that some poems worthy of inclusion may have been overlooked.

Spender's first collection, *Twenty Poems* (1930), was printed privately by Basil Blackwell in Oxford. Eleven of these poems were reproduced in his first volume for Faber and Faber, *Poems* (1933), and the others may be found in the section '1930–1934.'

I have prioritised *Poems* (1933) rather than the 1934 expanded edition in order to preserve the thematic development of the original volume. I have also restored the dedication to Christopher Isherwood, which perhaps requires some justification. Spender had inscribed his debut Faber and Faber volume to Isherwood, but withdrew the gesture shortly before publication when the two friends fell out. The rift was short-lived and Spender restored the dedication at the earliest opportunity, which was the edition of 1934. I believe I am honouring Spender's intentions, and the friendship, by allowing the original dedication to stand.

I am grateful to Lady Spender and Professor John Sutherland for invaluable advice and support while preparing the text; and to Paul Keegan and Matthew Hollis at Faber and Faber for initiating this edition.

MICHAEL BRETT

POEMS (1933)

To Christopher Isherwood

I

He will watch the hawk with an indifferent eye
        Or pitifully;
Nor on those eagles that so feared him, now
        Will strain his brow;
Weapons men use, stone, sling and strong-thewed bow
        He will not know.

This aristocrat, superb of all instinct,
        With death close linked
Had paced the enormous cloud, almost had won
        War on the sun;
Till now, like Icarus mid-ocean-drowned,
        Hands, wings, are found.

II

Rolled over on Europe: the sharp dew frozen to stars
Below us: above our heads the night
Frozen again to stars: the stars
In pools between our coats, and that charmed moon:
Ah, what supports? What cross draws out our arms
Heaves up our bodies towards the wind
And hammers us between the mirrored lights?

Only my body is real: which wolves
Are free to oppress and gnaw. Only this rose
My friend laid on my breast, and these few lines
Written from home, are real.

III

Marston, dropping it in the grate, broke his pipe.
Nothing hung on this act, it was no symbol
Ludicrous for calamity, but merely ludicrous.

That heavy-wrought briar with the great pine face
Now split across like a boxer's hanging dream
Of punishing a nigger, he brought from the continent;
It was his absurd relic, like bones,
Of stamping on the white-faced mountains,
Early beds in huts, and other journeys.

To hold the banks of the Danube, the slow barges down
   the river,
Those coracles with faces painted on,
Demanded his last money,
A foodless journey home, as pilgrimage.

IV

Not to you I sighed. No, not a word.
We climbed together. Any feeling was
Formed with the hills. It was like trees' unheard
And monumental sign of country peace.

But next day stumbling, panting up dark stairs,
Rushing in room and door flung wide, I knew.
Oh empty walls, book-carcases, blank chairs
All splintered in my head and cried for you.

V

Acts passed beyond the boundary of mere wishing
Not privy looks, hedged words, at times you saw.
These blundering, heart-surrendered troopers were
Small presents made, and waiting for the tram.

Then once you said 'Waiting was very kind'
And looked surprised: surprising for me too
Whose every movement had been missionary,
A pleading tongue unheard. I had not thought
That you, who nothing else saw, would see this.

So 'very kind' was merest overflow
Something I had not reckoned in myself,
A chance deserter from my force. When we touched hands
I felt the whole rebel, feared mutiny
And turned away,
Thinking, if these were tricklings through a dam,
I must have love enough to run a factory on,
Or give a city power, or drive a train.

VI

I hear the cries of evening, while the paw
Of dark creeps up the turf;
Sheep's bleating, swaying gulls' cry, the rook's caw,
The hammering surf.

I am inconstant yet this constancy
Of natural rest twangs at my heart;
Town-bred, I feel the roots of each earth-cry
Tear me apart.

These are the creakings of the dusty day
When the dog night bites sharp,
These fingers grip my soul and tear away
And pluck me like a harp.

I feel this huge sphere turn, the great wheel sing
While beasts move to their ease:
Sheep's love, gulls' peace – I feel my chattering
Uncared by these.

VII

Different living is not living in different places
But creating in the mind a map
Creating in the mind a desert
An isolated mountain or a kinder health-resort.

When I frowned, creating desert, Time only
Shook once his rigid column, as when Ape
Centuries before, with furrowed hand
Grabbed at stone, discerning a new use:
Putting a notch against the mind's progress:
Shaking Time, but with no change of Place.

VIII

An 'I' can never be great man.
This known great one has weakness
To friends is most remarkable for weakness
His ill-temper at meals, his dislike of being contradicted,
His only real pleasure fishing in ponds,
His only real desire – forgetting.

To advance from friends to the composite self
Central 'I' is surrounded by 'I eating',
'I loving', 'I angry', 'I excreting',
And the 'great I' planted in him
Has nothing to do with all these,

It can never claim its true place
Resting in the forehead, and secure in his gaze.
The 'great I' is an unfortunate intruder
Quarrelling with 'I tiring' and 'I sleeping'
And all those other 'I's who long for 'We dying'.

IX Beethoven's Death Mask

I imagine him still with heavy brow.
Huge, black, with bent head and falling hair
He ploughs the landscape. His face
Is this hanging mask transfigured,
This mask of death which the white lights make stare.

I see the thick hands clasped; the scare-crow coat;
The light strike upwards at the holes for eyes;
The beast squat in that mouth, whose opening is
The hollow opening of an organ pipe:
There the wind sings and the harsh longing cries.

He moves across my vision like a ship.
What else is iron but he? The fields divide
And, heaving, are changing waters of the sea.
He is prisoned, masked, shut off from being;
Life like a fountain he sees leap – outside.

Yet, in that head there twists the roaring cloud
And coils, as in a shell, the roaring wave.
The damp leaves whisper; bending to the rain
The April rises in him, chokes his lungs
And climbs the torturing passage of his brain.

Then the drums move away, the Distance shows;
Now cloudy peaks are bared; the mystic One
Horizons haze, as the blue incense heaven.
Peace, peace . . . Then splitting skull and dream, there comes,
Blotting our lights, the trumpeter, the sun.

X

Never being, but always at the edge of Being
My head, like Death-mask is brought into the sun.

The shadow pointing finger across cheek,
I move lips for tasting, I move hands for touching,
But never am nearer than touching
Though the spirit lean outward for seeing.
Observing rose, gold, eyes, an admired landscape,
My senses record the act of wishing,
Wishing to be
Rose, gold, landscape or another.
I claim fulfilment in the fact of loving.

XI

My parents quarrel in the neighbour room.
'How did you sleep last night?' 'I woke at four
To hear the wind that sulks along the floor
Blowing up dust like ashes from the tomb.'

'I was awake at three.' 'I heard the moth
Breed perilous worms.' 'I wept
All night, watching your rest.' 'I never slept
Nor sleep at all.' Thus ghastly they speak, both.

How can they sleep, who eat upon their fear
And watch their dreadful love fade as it grows?
Their life flowers, like an antique lovers' rose
Set puff'd and spreading in the chemist's jar.

I am your son, and from bad dreams arise.
My sight is fixed with horror, as I pass
Before the transitory glass
And watch the fungus cover up my eyes.

XII

My parents kept me from children who were rough
And who threw words like stones and who wore torn clothes.

Their thighs showed through rags. They ran in the street
And climbed cliffs and stripped by the country streams.

I feared more than tigers their muscles like iron
And their jerking hands and their knees tight on my arms.
I feared the salt coarse pointing of those boys
Who copied my lisp behind me on the road.

They were lithe, they sprang out behind hedges
Like dogs to bark at our world. They threw mud
And I looked another way, pretending to smile.
I longed to forgive them, yet they never smiled.

XIII

What I expected was
Thunder, fighting,
Long struggles with men
And climbing.
After continual straining
I should grow strong;
Then the rocks would shake
And I should rest long.

What I had not foreseen
Was the gradual day
Weakening the will
Leaking the brightness away,
The lack of good to touch
The fading of body and soul
Like smoke before wind
Corrupt, unsubstantial.

The wearing of Time,
And the watching of cripples pass
With limbs shaped like questions
In their odd twist,

The pulverous grief
Melting the bones with pity,
The sick falling from earth –
These, I could not foresee.

For I had expected always
Some brightness to hold in trust,
Some final innocence
To save from dust;
That, hanging solid,
Would dangle through all
Like the created poem
Or the dazzling crystal.

XIV In 1929

A whim of Time, the general arbiter,
Proclaims the love instead of death of friends.
Under the domed sky and athletic sun
The three stand naked: the new, bronzed German,
The communist clerk, and myself, being English.

Yet to unwind the travelled sphere twelve years
Then two take arms, spring to a ghostly posture.
Or else roll on the thing a further ten
And this poor clerk with world-offended eyes
Builds with red hands his heaven; makes our bones
The necessary scaffolding to peace.

*

Now I suppose that the once-envious dead
Have learnt a strict philosophy of clay
After these centuries, to haunt us no longer
In the churchyard or at the end of the lane
Or howling at the edge of the city
Beyond the last beanrows, near the new factory.

Our fathers killed. And yet there lives no feud
Like prompting Hamlet on the castle stair;
There falls no shade across our blank of peace,
We being together, struck across our path,
Or taper finger threatening solitude.

Our fathers' misery, the dead man's mercy,
The cynic's mystery, weave a philosophy
That the history of man traced purely from dust
Was lipping skulls on the revolving rim
Or the posture of genius with the granite head bowed:

Lives risen a moment, joined or separate,
Fall heavily, then are always separate,
A stratum unreckoned by geologists,
Sod lifted, turned, slapped back again with spade.

XV The Port

Hopelessly wound round with the cords of street
Men wander down their lines of level graves.
Sometimes the maze knots into flaring caves
Where magic-lantern faces skew for greeting.
Smile dawns with a harsh lightning, there's no speaking
And, far from lapping laughter, all's parched and hard.
Here the pale lily boys flaunt their bright lips,
Such pretty cups for money, and older whores
Skuttle rat-toothed into the dark outdoors.

Northwards the sea exerts his huge mandate.
His guardians, candles stand, the furnace beam,
Blinking pharos, and ringing from the yards.
In their fat gardens the merchants dwell, Southwards.
Well-fed, well-lit, well-spoken men are these,
With bronze-faced sons, and happy in their daughters.

XVI

Moving through the silent crowd
Who stand behind dull cigarettes
These men who idle in the road,
I have the sense of falling light.

They lounge at corners of the street
And greet friends with a shrug of shoulder
And turn their empty pockets out,
The cynical gestures of the poor.

Now they've no work, like better men
Who sit at desks and take much pay
They sleep long nights and rise at ten
To watch the hours that drain away.

I'm jealous of the weeping hours
They stare through with such hungry eyes.
I'm haunted by these images,
I'm haunted by their emptiness.

XVII

Who live under the shadow of a war,
What can I do that matters?
My pen stops, and my laughter, dancing, stop
Or ride to a gap.

How often, on the powerful crest of pride,
I am shot with thought
That halts the untamed horses of the blood,
The grip on good.

That moving whimpering and mating bear
Tunes to deaf ears:
Stuffed with the realer passions of the earth
Beneath this hearth.

XVIII

How strangely this sun reminds me of my love!
Of my walk alone at evening, when like the cottage smoke
Hope vanished, written amongst red wastes of sky.
I remember my strained listening to his voice
My staring at his face and taking the photograph
With the river behind and the woods touched by Spring;
Till the identification of a morning –
Expansive sheets of blue rising from fields
Roaring movements of light observed under shadow –
With his figure leaning over a map, is now complete.

What is left of that smoke which the wind blew away?
I corrupted his confidence and his sunlike happiness
So that even now in his turning of bolts or driving a machine
His hand will show error. That is for him.
For me this memory which now I behold,
When, from the pasturage, azure rounds me in rings
And the lark ascends, and his voice still rings, still rings.

XIX

Your body is stars whose million glitter here:
I am lost amongst the branches of this sky
Here near my breast, here in my nostrils, here
Where our vast arms like streams of fire lie.

How can this end? My healing fills the night
And hangs its flags in worlds I cannot near.
Our movements range through miles, and when we kiss
The moment widens to enclose long years.

*

Beholders of the promised dawn of truth
The explorers of immense and simple lines,

Here is our goal, men cried, but it was lost
Amongst the mountain mists and mountain pines.

So with this face of love, whose breathings are
A mystery shadowed on the desert floor:
The promise hangs, this swarm of stars and flowers,
And then there comes the shutting of a door.

XX The Prisoners

Far far the least of all, in want,
Are these,
The prisoners
Turned massive with their vaults and dark with dark.

They raise no hands, which rest upon their knees,
But lean their solid eyes against the night,
Dimly they feel
Only the furniture they use in cells.

Their Time is almost Death. The silted flow
Of years on years
Is marked by dawns
As faint as cracks on mud-flats of despair.

My pity moves amongst them like a breeze
On walls of stone
Fretting for summer leaves, or like a tune
On ears of stone.

Then, when I raise my hands to strike,
It is too late,
There are no chains that fall
Nor visionary liquid door
Melted with anger.

When have their lives been free from walls and dark
And airs that choke?

And where less prisoner to let my anger
Like a sun strike?

If I could follow them from room to womb
To plant some hope
Through the black silk of the big-bellied gown
There would I win.

No, no, no,
It is too late for anger,
Nothing prevails
But pity for the grief they cannot feel.

XXI

Without that once clear aim, the path of flight
To follow for a life-time through white air,
This century chokes me under roots of night,
I suffer like history in Dark Ages, where
Truth lies in dungeons, from which drifts no whisper:
We hear of towers long broken off from sight
And tortures and war, in dark and smoky rumour,
But on men's buried lives there falls no light.
Watch me who walk through coiling streets where rain
And fog drown every cry: at corners of day
Road drills explore new areas of pain,
Nor summer nor light may reach down here to play.
The city builds its horror in my brain,
This writing is my only wings away.

XXII

oh young men oh young comrades
it is too late now to stay in those houses
your fathers built where they built you to build to breed

money on money –   it is too late
to make or even to count what has been made
Count rather those fabulous possessions
which begin with your body and your fiery soul:–
the hairs on your head the muscles extending
in ranges with their lakes across your limbs
Count your eyes as jewels and your valued sex
then count the sun and the innumerable coined light
sparkling on waves and spangled under trees
It is too late to stay in great houses where the ghosts are
    prisoned
– those ladies like flies perfect in amber
those financiers like fossils of bones in coal.
Oh comrades, step beautifully from the solid wall
advance to rebuild and sleep with friend on hill
advance to rebel and remember what you have
no ghost ever had, immured in his hall.

XXIII

I think continually of those who were truly great.
Who, from the womb, remembered the soul's history
Through corridors of light where the hours are suns,
Endless and singing. Whose lovely ambition
Was that their lips, still touched with fire,
Should tell of the Spirit clothed from head to foot in song.
And who hoarded from the Spring branches
The desires falling across their bodies like blossoms.

What is precious is never to forget
The essential delight of the blood drawn from ageless springs
Breaking through rocks in worlds before our earth.
Never to deny its pleasure in the morning simple light
Nor its grave evening demand for love.
Never to allow gradually the traffic to smother
With noise and fog, the flowering of the spirit.

Near the snow, near the sun, in the highest fields
See how these names are fêted by the waving grass
And by the streamers of white cloud
And whispers of wind in the listening sky.
The names of those who in their lives fought for life,
Who wore at their hearts the fire's centre.
Born of the sun, they travelled a short while towards the
    sun,
And left the vivid air signed with their honour.

XXIV

After they have tired of the brilliance of cities
And of striving for office where at last they may languish
Hung round with easy chains until
Death and Jerusalem glorify also the crossing-sweeper:
Then those streets the rich built and their easy love
Fade like old cloths, and it is death stalks through life
Grinning white through all faces
Clean and equal like the shine from snow.

In this time when grief pours freezing over us,
When the hard light of pain gleams at every street corner,
When those who were pillars of that day's gold roof
Shrink in their clothes; surely from hunger
We may strike fire, like fire from flint?
And our strength is now the strength of our bones
Clean and equal like the shine from snow
And the strength of famine and of our enforced idleness,
And it is the strength of our love for each other.

Readers of this strange language,
We have come at last to a country
Where light equal, like the shine from snow, strikes all faces,
Here you may wonder

How it was that works, money, interest, building, could ever
    hide
The palpable and obvious love of man for man.

Oh comrades, let not those who follow after
– The beautiful generation that shall spring from our sides –
Let not them wonder how after the failure of banks,
The failure of cathedrals and the declared insanity of our
    rulers,
We lacked the Spring-like resources of the tiger
Or of plants who strike out new roots to gushing waters.
But through torn-down portions of old fabric let their eyes
Watch the admiring dawn explode like a shell
Around us, dazing us with its light like snow.

XXV The Funeral

Death is another milestone on their way.
With laughter on their lips and with winds blowing round
    them
They record simply
How this one excelled all others in making driving belts.

This is festivity, it is the time of statistics
When they record what one unit contributed:
They are glad as they lay him back in the earth
And thank him for what he gave them.

They walk home remembering the straining red flags,
And with pennons of song still fluttering through their blood
They speak of the world state
With its towns like brain-centres and its pulsing arteries.

They think how one life hums, revolves and toils,
One cog in a golden and singing hive:
Like spark from fire, its task happily achieved,
It falls away quietly.

No more are they haunted by the individual grief
Nor the crocodile tears of European genius,
The decline of a culture
Mourned by scholars who dream of the ghosts of Greek
   boys.

XXVI The Express

After the first powerful plain manifesto
The black statement of pistons, without more fuss
But gliding like a queen, she leaves the station.
Without bowing and with restrained unconcern
She passes the houses which humbly crowd outside,
The gasworks and at last the heavy page
Of death, printed by gravestones in the cemetery.
Beyond the town there lies the open country
Where, gathering speed, she acquires mystery,
The luminous self-possession of ships on ocean.
It is now she begins to sing – at first quite low
Then loud, and at last with a jazzy madness –
The song of her whistle screaming at curves,
Of deafening tunnels, brakes, innumerable bolts.
And always light, aerial, underneath
Goes the elate metre of her wheels.
Steaming through metal landscape on her lines
She plunges new eras of wild happiness
Where speed throws up strange shapes, broad curves
And parallels clean like the steel of guns.
At last, further than Edinburgh or Rome,
Beyond the crest of the world, she reaches night
Where only a low streamline brightness
Of phosphorus on the tossing hills is white.
Ah, like a comet through flame, she moves entranced
Wrapt in her music no bird song, no, nor bough
Breaking with honey buds, shall ever equal.

XXVII The Landscape near an Aerodrome

More beautiful and soft than any moth
With burring furred antennae feeling its huge path
Through dusk, the air-liner with shut-off engines
Glides over suburbs and the sleeves set trailing tall
To point the wind. Gently, broadly, she falls
Scarcely disturbing charted currents of air.

Lulled by descent, the travellers across sea
And across feminine land indulging its easy limbs
In miles of softness, now let their eyes trained by watching
Penetrate through dusk the outskirts of this town
Here where industry shows a fraying edge.
Here they may see what is being done.

Beyond the winking masthead light
And the landing-ground, they observe the outposts
Of work: chimneys like lank black fingers
Or figures frightening and mad: and squat buildings
With their strange air behind trees, like women's faces
Shattered by grief. Here where few houses
Moan with faint light behind their blinds
They remark the unhomely sense of complaint, like a dog
Shut out and shivering at the foreign moon.

In the last sweep of love, they pass over fields
Behind the aerodrome, where boys play all day
Hacking dead grass: whose cries, like wild birds,
Settle upon the nearest roofs
But soon are hid under the loud city.

Then, as they land, they hear the tolling bell
Reaching across the landscape of hysteria
To where, larger than all the charcoaled batteries
And imaged towers against that dying sky,
Religion stands, the church blocking the sun.

XXVIII The Pylons

The secret of these hills was stone, and cottages
Of that stone made,
And crumbling roads
That turned on sudden hidden villages.

Now over these small hills they have built the concrete
That trails black wire:
Pylons, those pillars
Bare like nude, giant girls that have no secret.

The valley with its gilt and evening look
And the green chestnut
Of customary root
Are mocked dry like the parched bed of a brook.

But far above and far as sight endures
Like whips of anger
With lightning's danger
There runs the quick perspective of the future.

This dwarfs our emerald country by its trek
So tall with prophecy:
Dreaming of cities
Where often clouds shall lean their swan-white neck.

XXIX

Abrupt and charming mover,
Your pointed eyes under lit leaves,
Your light hair, your smile,
I watch burn in a land
Bright in the cave of night
And protected by my hand.

Beneath the ribs, in Jonah's whale,
All night I hold you: from day
I have recalled your play
Disturbing as birds' flying
And with the Spring's infection
And denial of satisfaction.

You dance, forgetting all: in joy
Sustaining that instant of the eye
Which like a flaming wheel can be:
Your games of cards, hockey with toughs,
Winking at girls, shoes cribbed from toffs,
Like the encircling summer dew
Glaze me from head to toe.

By night I hold you, but by day
I watch you weave the silk cocoon
Of a son's, or a skater's, play:
We have no meeting place
Beneath that dancing, glassy surface:
The outward figure of delight
Creates no warm and sanguine image
Answering my language.

XXX

In railway halls, on pavements near the traffic,
They beg, their eyes made big by empty staring
And only measuring Time, like the blank clock.

No, I shall weave no tracery of pen-ornament
To make them birds upon my singing-tree:
Time merely drives these lives which do not live
As tides push rotten stuff along the shore.

– There is no consolation, no, none
In the curving beauty of that line

Traced on our graphs through history, where the
    oppressor
Starves and deprives the poor.

Paint here no draped despairs, no saddening clouds
Where the soul rests, proclaims eternity.
But let the wrong cry out as raw as wounds
This Time forgets and never heals, far less transcends.

XXXI

Those fireballs, those ashes,
Those cloudbursts, those whirling madman hurricanes
The palatial sky breathes, make men's organic change.
Some, extinguished by horror, leap into the thinnest air,
Inevitable delight is theirs, no sweeter delight
Than to be keener than knives, invisible to run
Around the endless earth, for ever to blow upon
The lips of their loved friends.
Others shake in bed whilst the sorrowing elements
Twist them to shapes of dreadful grief,
Only the mirror knows their traitorous joy.
Man must rejoice, misfortune cannot fall,
Him I delight in accepts joy as joy;
He is richened by sorrow as a river by its bends,
He is the swallower of fire,
His bowels are molten fire; when he leaves his friend
He takes pleasure in icy solitude; he is the dandy;
He is the swimmer, waves only lift him higher,
He is the rose, sultry loveliness does not oppress him;
The clouds of our obscuring disillusion
Are thoughts which shade his brow, and then he smiles.
I stand far from him, but I wish that these
Slanting iron hail pattern no stigmata
Showing me sadder than those poor, and rarer.

Let the elements that fall make me of finer mixture
Not struck from sorrow, but vast joys, and learning laughter.

XXXII

From all these events, from the slump, from the war, from the
    boom,
From the Italian holiday, from the skirring
Of the revolving light for an adventurer,
From the crowds in the square at dusk, from the shooting,
From the loving, from the dying, however we prosper in death
Whether lying under twin lilies and branched candles
Or stiffened on the pavement like a frozen sack, hidden
From night and peace by the lamps:
From all these events, Time solitary will emerge
Like a rocket bursting from mist: above the trouble,
Untangled with our pasts, be sure Time will leave us.

At first growing up in us more nakedly than our own nature,
Driving us beyond what seemed the final choking swamp,
Ruin, the all-covering illness, to a new and empty air;
Singling us from the war which killed ten millions;
Carrying us elate through the happy summer fields;
Nesting us in high rooms of a house where voices
Murmured at night from the garden, as if flowering from
    water;
Then sending us to lean days after the years of fulfilment;
At last dropping us into the hard, bright crater of the dead.

Our universal ally, but larger than our purpose, whose flanks
Stretch to planets unknown in our brief, particular battle,
Tomorrow Time's progress will forget us even here,
When our bodies are rejected like the beetle's shard, today
Already, now, we are forgotten on those stellar shores.
Time's ambition, huge as space, will hang its flags
In distant worlds, and in years on this world as distant.

XXXIII

Not palaces, an era's crown
Where the mind dwells, intrigues, rests;
The architectural gold-leaved flower
From people ordered like a single mind,
I build. This only what I tell:
It is too late for rare accumulation,
For family pride, for beauty's filtered dusts;
I say, stamping the words with emphasis,
Drink from here energy and only energy,
As from the electric charge of a battery,
To will this Time's change.
Eye, gazelle, delicate wanderer,
Drinker of horizon's fluid line;
Ear that suspends on a chord
The spirit drinking timelessness;
Touch, love, all senses;
Leave your gardens, your singing feasts,
Your dreams of suns circling before our sun,
Of heaven after our world.
Instead, watch images of flashing brass
That strike the outward sense, the polished will,
Flag of our purpose which the wind engraves.
No spirit seek here rest. But this: No man
Shall hunger: Man shall spend equally.
Our goal which we compel: Man shall be man.

– That programme of the antique Satan
Bristling with guns on the indented page,
With battleship towering from hilly waves:
For what? Drive of a ruining purpose
Destroying all but its age-long exploiters.
Our programme like this, yet opposite,
Death to the killers, bringing light to life.

1930–1934

The Dust Made Flesh

These dust made grass I also turned to flesh.

First made I Marston the superb boxer
More than with men who dealt with death,
Marston who skied through snow,
Curved through the whiteness, ran,
Helmeted drove through air,
– A balanced winner backed by all the crowd,
Often portrayed in travellers' photographs.
Then Helen, the astonishing hostess,
Dark-eyed, words piercing night like stars,
With fine hands, I formed. Came Catherine
Third, who despised me even when in womb,
Too insolent for the earth she sprang in sky,
Along the ice-fleeced rocks shot chamois down.
Last I conceived
Ainger the poet, severe, voiced raucous-reed,
With fascinating facets of crude mind,
An enormous percipient mass on the plain.

These made, these loved I: the four fixed like rocks
On Europe.

                Across the frozen map
Winters weave frost, the old dust-patterns change.
A lake cracks its surface. The winds
– Black bears – haunt dreadful corners.
Cataract in our eyes, the vultures come.

These made, these loved again their souls arise,
Marston his brows bound up with Athens
– A runner still is running past my house.

The stars nurse Helen, thousands like gloved hands.
Her perpetual saxophone
Sister to winds that scratch across the moon
Cries 'Catherine.' Ainger reports
With sullen voice the growth of other graves,
But these . . .

These are not grass or thrust into a furnace.

His Figure Passes

His figure passes, and I confess
No suddenness of pain, but an old pain
More constant in the heart that heart lives by
Again revived: as though from happiness,
Freshness of wind and the cloud-breathing sky,
All happiness rolled away – again revealed
That sore and flaming wheel I must live by.

'Hearing from its cage'

Hearing from its cage
Lion that roars the traffic down,
Or seeing the rash sun
Strike out the fog, brings him.

For he was constant April
All times and everywhere;
Like the straight, cherished deer
By pride fenced from the people.

And seeing a new god
Dropped from the sky, no less
Calls out on timelessness
Than seeing where he trod.

The gross crowd and the winter
Were choked back with surprise
At the sun trapped in his eyes,
At his nostrils' curved adventure.

And he was one so gentle
He could take royally
The bowing of gold cities,
The stooping of the temple.

And where his form passed by
Grass would have tongues for truth,
Stones would speak words of truth.
And these words cannot die.

'Lying awake at night'

Lying awake at night
Shows again the difference
Between me, and his innocence.
I vow he was born of light
    And that dark gradually
    Closed each eye,
He woke, he sleeps so naturally.

So, born of nature, amongst men most divine,
He copied, and was our sun.
    And his mood was thunder
    For anger,
But mostly a calm, English one.

Constant April

You that were constant April
    Received me for five days.

With April sky always,
Five clear bells from a steeple.

And, when you laughed, your laughter
Was like the bright cascade
The sun sheds on a cloud,
With its faint shadow after.

And, if you frowned, your frowning
Was knit as light as these
Slight showers, that shake the trees
And gleam across the morning.

'Saying "Good morning" becomes painful'

Saying 'Good morning' becomes painful
And talking at meals, since slight words
Fall cumbrously about our feet, like swords.
Hours we've braved out together through a lull
And then word for word we've faced the storm;
At such times I have made conversation,
Speaking across tables, a form of possession
Like taking your wrists and feeling your lips warm.

But chance 'Good mornings,' seeing you in the street,
Talking at the door, or when each starts
Looks eye to eye and then breaks eyes away,
Is more than I can stand. We should not meet
So lightly. Let us break our hearts
Not casually, but on a stated day.

Always between Hope and Fear

Soul, swaying between hope and fear,
First radiant and leaping, then pallid and trembling,

Always plunging the future
Always to what is near,

Now now be at peace,
Cancel that heaven and that abyss
Whose blues and reds roar back to madness,
Avoid these chasms and steep gaps in space.

Sense should grope on all fours, not driven
By pleasure or horror assailing like the wind,
Not giddied by stars, but touching the ground,
Not struggling through flame to the imagined heaven.

The Swan

The trumpets were curled away, the drum beat no more.
Only the Swan the Swan danced in my brain:
All night she spun; dropped, lifted again,
Arched and curved her arms; sunk on the frore
Snow-brittle feathers skirting her; reclined on hands
Buckling her waist, where the moon glanced.
How small her waist was, and the feet that danced!

Sometimes she bent back, and a breeze fanned
Her hair that touched the ground, and, shown
Between her Swan's legs, feathers and white down.

'That girl who laughed and had black eyes'

That girl who laughed and had black eyes
Spoke here ten days ago. She smiles
Still in my thought; the lip still promises
The body lives, and the quick eye beguiles.

Now that she's dead, I feel the living flame
Move across walls and twist across my sight:

Through tilting, smothering waters of Death's name,
Through the transparent grave, I see her bright.

She lives beneath our common objects, dust
And chairs, and her few poems about the room.
Although death play its tricks, and the earth's crust
Swallow her up in the enormous tomb,

I meet her every turn; the muffled part
The stilled applause, the pageant to appal,
Startle her shade to take birth in my heart:
I see her dancing through the solid wall!

from POEMS (1934)

VI

At the end of two months' holiday there came a night
When I lay awake and the sea's distant fretless scansion
By imagination scourged rose to a fight
Like the town's roar, pouring out apprehension.
I was in a train. Like the quick spool of a film
I watched hasten away the simple green which can heal
All sadness. Abruptly the sign *Ferry to Wilm*
And the cottage by the lake, were vivid, but unreal.
    Real were iron lines, and, smashing the grass.
The cars in which we ride, and real our compelled time:
Painted on enamel beneath the moving glass.
Unreal were cows, the wave-winged storks, the lime:
These burned in a clear world from which we pass
Like *rose* and *love* in a forgotten rhyme.

XII

After success, your little afternoon success,
You watch jealous perplexity mould my head
To the shape of a dark and taloned bird
And fix claws in my lungs, and then you pass
Your silk soothing hand across my arm
And smile; I look at you, and through as if through glass,
And do not say 'You lie'. There is something in you
Less visible than glass or else it is
A void imagination fills with pities.
You and that famous whore and the thief
Are simple still, I think: you trust belief
Of the lean spectator living on illusion.

This delicate smile that strokes my arm I cannot
Break. It is your truth's invisible creation.

XIII

Alas, when he laughs it is not he:
But a shopwalker who scrapes his hands, and bows,
Seller of ties and shirts who shows his teeth
Even out of hours. Sometimes a flickering regret
For these damp, too-generous ruined gestures
Burns in his eyes. If he himself could laugh
To match his light and naked hair
And the jungle still glimmering beneath his lashes,
I think that obdurate cliff
That shuts out all our sky and always grows
Black between us and the silent pools of the will
Would fall: and that the rocks
Would burst with German streams again.

XIX

Shapes of death haunt life,
Neurosis eclipsing each in special shadow:
Unrequited love, not solving
The need to become another's body
Wears black invisibility:
The greed for property
Heaps a skyscraper over the breathing ribs:
The speedlines of dictators
Cut their own stalks:
From afar, we watch the best of us –
Whose adored desire was to die for the world.

Ambition is my death. That flat thin flame
I feed, that plants my shadow. This prevents love

And offers love of being loved or loving.
The humorous self-forgetful drunkenness
It hates, demands the pyramids
Be built. Who can prevent
His death's industry, which when he sleeps
Throws up its towers? And conceals in slackness
The dreams of revolution, the birth of death?

Also the swallows by autumnal instinct
Comfort us with their effortless exhaustion
In great unguided flight to their complete South.
There on my fancied pyramids they lodge
But for delight, their whole compulsion.
Not teaching me to love, but soothing my eyes;
Not saving me from death, but saving me for speech.

XXII For T.A.R.H.

Even whilst I watch him I am remembering
The quick laugh of the wasp gold eyes.
The column turning from the staring pane
Even while I see I remember, for love
Is soaked in memory and says
I have seen what I see, and I wear
All pasts and futures like a doomed, domed sky.
Thus I wear always the glint of quick lids
And the blue axel turning; these shall be
Fixed in a night that knows and sees
The equable currents.

At night my life lies with no past nor future
But only space. It watches
Hope and despair and the small vivid longings
Like minnows gnaw the body. Where it drank love
It lives in sameness. Here are
Gestures indelible. The wiry copper hair

And the mothlike lips at dusk and that human
Glance, which makes the sun forgotten.

XXIV Van der Lubbe

O staring eyes, searchlight disks,
Listen at my lips. I am louder than to
Swim an inhuman channel, be boy, or climb
A town's notorious mast.

I throw you these words, I care not which I tear,
You must eat my scraps and dance.
I am glad I am glad that this people is mad:
Their eyes must drink my newspaper glance.

Why do you laugh? Sombre Judge asks.
I laugh at this trial, although it shall make
My life end at a dazzling steel gate,
Axe severing a stalk.

Yes, no, yes, no. Shall I tell you what I know?
Not to Goering, but, dear movietone, I whisper it to you.
I laugh because my laughter
Is like justice, twisted by a howitzer.

The senses are shaken from the judging heart:
The eye turned backwards and the outside world
Into the grave of the skull rolled:
With no stars riding heaven, and disparate.

The spitting at justice, the delight of mere guns
Exploding the trees, where in their branches
Truth greenly balances, are what I am
Who die with the dead and slobber with fun.

XXVI

Passing, men are sorry for the birds in cages
And for constricted nature hedged and lined,
But what do they say to your pleasant bird
Physical delight, since years tamed?

Behind centuries, behind the continual hill,
The wood you felled, your clothes, the slums you built,
Only love knows where that bird dips his head,
Only the sun, soaked in memory, flashes on his neck.

Dance, will you? And sing? Yet pray he is dead,
Invent politics to hide him and law suits and suits:
Now he's impossible and quite destroyed like grass
Where the fields are covered with your more living houses.

I never hear you are happy, but I wonder
Whether it was at a shiny bazaar,
At a brittle dance or a party, that you could create
Procrastination of nature, for your talk and laughter are
Only a glass that flashes back the light
And that covers only hate.

Will you not forgive him? I have signed his release
Alarming and gentle like the blood's throb,
And his fountain of joy wakes the solitary stag
From his cherished sleep.

But if you still bar your pretty bird, remember
Revenge and despair are prisoned in your bowels.
Life cannot pardon the ideal without scruple,
The enemy of flesh, the angel and destroyer,
Creator of a martyrdom serene, but horrible.

XXX Perhaps

The explosion of a bomb
the submarine – a burst bubble filled with water –
the chancellor clutching his shot arm (and that was Perhaps
a put-up job for their own photographers)
the parliament their own side set afire
and then our party forbidden
and the mine flooded, an accident I hope.

motorcycles wires aeroplanes cars trains
converging at that one town Geneva
top-hats talking at edge of crystal healing lake
then mountains.

We know this from rotating machines
from flanges stamping, cutting, sicking out sheets from paper
    rolls.
The newsmen run like points of compass: their arms are
gusts that carry sheets of mouldy paper:
our eyes mud those scraps rub on.

In his skidding car he wonders
when watching landscape attack him
'is it rushing (I cannot grasp it) or is it
at rest with its own silence I cannot touch?'

Was that final when they shot him? did that war
lop our dead branches? are my new leaves splendid?
is it leviathan, that revolution
hugely nosing at edge of antarctic?

only Perhaps. Can be that we grow smaller
donnish and bony shut in our racing prison:
headlines are walls that shake and close
the dry dice rattled in their wooden box.

Can be deception of things only changing. Out there
perhaps growth of humanity above the plain

hangs: not the timed explosion, oh but Time
monstrous with stillness like the Himalayan range.

XXXVIII New Year

Here at the centre of the turning year,
The turning Polar North,
The frozen streets, and the black fiery joy
Of the Child launched again forth,
I ask that all the years and years
Of future disappointment, like a snow
Chide me at one fall now.

I leave him who burns endlessly
In the brandy pudding crowned with holly,
And I ask that Time should freeze my skin
And all my fellow travellers harden
Who are not flattered by this town
Nor up its twenty storeys whirled
To prostitutes without infection.

Cloak us in accidents and in the failure
Of the high altar and marital adventure;
In family disgrace, denunciation
Of bankers, a premier's assassination.
From the government windows
Let heads of headlines watch depart,
Strangely depart by staying, those
Who build a new world in their heart.

Where scythe shall curve but not upon our neck
And lovers proceed to their forgetting work,
Answering the harvests of obliteration.
After the frozen years and streets
Our tempered will shall plough across the nations.
The engine hurrying through the lucky valley

The hand that moves to guide the silent lines
Effect their beauty without robbery.

Autumn Day

From the German of Rainer Maria Rilke

Lord, it is time. The summer was so huge.
Now lay your shadows on the sundials
And across the floor let the winds loose.

Command the last fruits to be fine;
Give to them yet two southerly days more;
Drive all their ripeness in and pour
The last sweet drop into the heavy wine.

Who now no home has, builds himself none more.
Who now alone is, he will stay so, long,
He will watch, read, write letters that are long
And through the avenues here and there
When the leaves run, restlessly wander.

[1933]

Orpheus Eurydice Hermes

After Rilke

That was the singular mine of souls.
Like still silver ores they went
as veins travelling its dark. Between roots
was the source of the blood that goes forth to men,
and heavy like porphyry it seemed in the dark.
Further, nothing red.

Rocks were there
and unreal woods. Bridges over voids

and yonder huge, grey, blind loch,
that over its far background hung
like rainy skies above a landscape.
And between meadows, of mild and full forbearance,
appeared the pale strip of the single road
laid in like a long pallor.

And on this single road they came.

Foremost the slender man in the blue mantle,
who stared in front of him, dumb and impatient.
Without chewing, his pace devoured the way
in great bites: his hands hung
heavy and clenched, out of the fall of folds.
And nothing more they knew of the light lyre,
which in the left had grown ingrown
like rose-tendrils in the olive tree bough.
And his senses were as if in two:
for whilst his glance ran before him like a dog,
turned round, went back and then away again
and waiting at the next corner stood –
his hearing hung back like an odour.
Sometimes it seemed to him as if it stretched
right to the walking of those other two,
who were to follow this whole climb.
At other times it was his climbing echo
only, and his mantle's draught, that were behind him.
He told himself, however, they'd surely come:
said it aloud, and heard his voice die away.
Indeed they'd come, only they were two
of terribly light going. Were he allowed
but once to turn (was not the looking back
sure dissolution of this entire labour,
now only being completed) he must see them,
the two soft-treading, who silently follow him:
the god of journeys and of far embassy,
with travelling cap over fair eyes,

43

carrying the slender rod before his body
and with wings fluttering at his ankles;
and given to his left hand – she.
She who was so much loved, that from a lyre
more lament came than from lamenting women:
and from lament a world was born, in which
all was recreated: wood and valley,
road, habitation, field and river and beast;
so that around this world of lament, just as
around the other earth a sun
and a star-set silent heaven went,
a heaven lamenting with distorted stars:
this one who was so much loved.

And still she walked, leaning on that god's hand,
her step narrowed by the long winding sheet,
uncertain, mild and without impatience.
She was closed in herself, like one with child,
and thought not of the man who went before her,
nor of the road, which climbed up into life.
She was shut in herself. Her being dead
filled her like fullness.
Like a fruit with sweetness and the dark
so was she full with her great death,
which still remained so new, that she grasped nothing.

She was in a new maidenhood, and
untouchable; her sex was closed
like a young flower towards the evening
and now her hands to marriage were
so much estranged, that even the light god's
endlessly gentle guiding touch
offended her like a too great intimacy.

She had already ceased to be that woman,
the blonde who echoed through the poet's songs,
no more was she the great bed's scent and island

and that man's property no more.
She was already loosened like long hair,
abandoned like the fallen rain
and portioned out like hundredfold provision.
She was already root
when precipitately
the god did stop her and with pain in his call
the words spoke: 'He has turned' –
she grasped nothing and whispered softly: 'Who?'
But far off, dark before the light way out,
someone stood, whose countenance
could not be recognized. He stood and saw
how along the strip of meadow path
with mournful glance the god of embassy
silently turned, following the figure
already walking back on this same road,
her step narrowed by the long winding sheet,
uncertain, mild and without impatience.

[1934]

45

VIENNA (1934)

To Muriel

They will be swift with swiftness of the tigress,
None will break ranks, though nations trek from progress.

Wilfred Owen

I Arrival at the City

Whether the man living or the man dying
Whether this man's dead life, or that man's life dying
His real life a fading light his real death a light growing.

Whether the live dead I live with. Ladies of the Pension
Beaurepas, their kind grey cropped love prattling
Amongst diseases. 'I think an operation
At the North Pole where this world is all white flesh
Is dear, if you love him.' And at the head of our table
Mister proprietor, oh our king and prime minister
Our wet dream dictator, our people's president
Printed in papers and cut out with scissors,
Dead man living, bald bobbing cork:
Thumping me on the back and saying: 'Old man,
Cheer up, stand up. . . . Frankly, would you have known
I wasn't English? . . . I thought not. When I acted
All through the 'States – hopped through the chorus girl
   ranks –
Way down mid West, they say "he's more English than the
   English".
Why, in Chicago. . . . Yes, more of a sportsman . . .
How much, how much did that tie cost?
How much, how much do you think I lost
What with the war and the inflation and what with our old
   picturesque estate gone? . . .
What do you earn? . . . Well, if you know Latin
You'll comprehend these festivities, *penis in circensem* . . .
Of course to a stranger like yourself, not habitué . . .
Have you a dark suit? . . . Well, that shirt *might* do . . .
I know she's a bitch, but quite my type. . . .'
Wing tie. Winged nose. A bleared, active eye.
The stick and strut of a sprucer day.

Whether this man's dead life stinking, like an open wound
   decaying,

Or the other's life sinking, and his real life decaying
His wound a wound, his life a life, his death
Opening to life like a flower him overarching –
Yes, the tube stuck in his stomach, and the rotten waste
Dripping in flasks; eyes red, jaw dropped, his mouth
A printed o; his kind hair flourishing
Wild above the wreck, like grass tall on a ruin;
Beard tufts from crannies of experience bristling.
Unroll this death, and flowers revive and rain
Like hair strokes on the faces of his girls.

Whether the man alive, or the man dying
If the live man is dead, if the dying man
Has life, though dying. And if this city
With statues of desirable angels
Whose tears are solid worlds; with palaces;
With songs buried beneath the ground like rotted leaves
To spring as cucumbers; has also its
Obscene electric gestures, its glance like rape
Hanging at doorways, I choose the wholly dead.
I hold their leathern hands. Their courtesy
Like lamps through orange fog, with a glazed eye
Can preach still. Here they nod and nod,
Their devout stone hair shitted by birds,
For birds still soothe them with a cooing prayer
Comforting as the starved appeal of beggars.

It is not death we fear but that a memory
Reported in our veins as absolute peace
And scrolled on buildings built by ancestors
Should turn an agonized, deathly face . . .
Now the past builds no peace, for harmless bombs
Ticking in bushes, shock us with their bangs,
Tearing anonymous limbs from senseless corpses.
The settled mountain, the background to our lives
Slides its burnt slopes, where legends told
Our parents walked with God. The puffs of smoke

At first as cool as fans, spread to a fog
And louder and louder the guns utter:
'How can we kill these dead? O, kill their worth.'

The part true to this town is a square quarter:
Unhomely windows, floors scrubbed clean of love,
A waste canvas sky, uniformed nuns,
Streets tinkling with the silver ambulance.
We breathe the bandaged air and watch through windows
Metal limbs, glass eyes, ourselves frozen on fires.

Unless indeed we stand upon a word,
Forgiveness, the brink of a renewing river . . .

A word, a brink, like the first uttered love.
Upon the pulsing throat springs the hot tiger.
Instantly released, in joy and sorrow they fall,
Escaping the whole world, two separate worlds of one,
Writing a new world with their figure 2.
Accepting the dreaded, the whispered happy postures
They dive into their dream with dreamed of gestures.

Not love, not death, not the dead living:
But cold cold as 'the will to alleviate
Certain material evils'.
                    The Time is
Dawn in the city with light dripping
On speechless pavement, on mirroring parallels
Of a surviving and dead wish, the defeated
Staring, white canal.
                    The Place meets
The Time: with difficult light creaking
To fill the streets up to the level roofs
To fill the morning, which is a dulled cistern.

Remote from drums . . .
                    The live ones are
Those who, going to work early, behold the world's

Utter margin where all is stone and iron,
And wrong. While the dead sleep
The bins are emptied, the streets washed of their dung,
The first trucks shunted; and the will emerges
On alteration. Alteration.

Whether the man living or the man dying,
Whether this man's dead life, or that man's life dying.

II Parade of the Executive

The Executive:

In order to create order, in order
To illustrate the truth that we are your ancestors
Let the generals wear their orders
Let the firemen dress like archdukes let the army
Be only one of six private armies
Let there be processions o let banners
Stream through the streets that anyhow look like pictures
Let no one disagree let Dollfuss
Fey, Starhemberg, the whole bloody lot
Appear frequently, shaking hands at street corners
Looking like bad sculptures of their photographs.
Let there be bands and stands and preparations
And grateful peasants in costumed deputations
Create the ghost of an emperor's coronation
Stalking the streets and holding up the trams.

The Unemployed:

Dispersed like idle points of a vague star:
Huddled on benches, nude at bathing places,
And made invisible by crucifying suns
Day after day, again with grief afire at night,
They do not watch what we show.

Their eyes are fixed upon an economic margin
Where the corn's starved by tares, where fluid grass
Trickles through rotted floors of senseless mills,
Where railway crossings with feeling, lifted wands
Are blistered, rails rust, bricks fall, and ivy
Smothers phallic chimneys.
                                        Ask the unemployed
At pavement's edge, at brink of river
Why do you stare at us with the same indifference
As at a main road of wheels and legs and facts
Birth, death, the inexplicable irrelevance
Of lust? (Do not ask that woman
With dark eyes neglected, a demanding turn of the head
And hair of black silky beasts, because our life is
A cage of lightest aluminium bars
Beyond the strength of tigers, conquering what's most feared
With moral weakness.) But turn to boys
Your bought lovers, howitzer fodder, blazoned
Future; why do you play cards
In gutters, sulk, hands in pocket, strip naked
And bathe, hike, betray your girls?
Is history ungrateful? Do books
Ignore us? Can a government be unimportant?

We can read their bodies like advertisements
On hoardings, shouting with common answers.
Not saying, life is happy, unhappy is ill,
Death is reward, law just, but only
Life is life, body is body, a day
Is the sun: there is left only beauty
Of merest being, of swimming, of somehow not starving:
And merest beauty has a sun-tanned body
Available for uses, but only sold. Pathic
Strength of marble thighs, Greek chest, a torso
Without purposive veins travelling to hands.
'It is a daystream thick with many

Laws, bombs, processions, handbills, church services,
Straws doubtless golden float among the many
But are indiscernible to a rich eye,
A drowned eye.' Politely, they stay away.

   The Executive:

A fine show we offer on a windy day
May 27th: flags like whippets tugging, 4 loud speakers
Over the baroque porch, blowing our gilt trumpets.
Seated below, Major Fey's 'strong' white face,
A wet handkerchief shot through with two lead bullets.
Dr Dollfuss with his daughter; smiling, smiling.
The speeches, the photographs, the Grand Mass, and the
   volleys
Of gunfire hammered with Holy Ghost, hammered
Into the steel of barrels, of rifles, of howitzers.
Ministerial lips smile, but what's transparent
As thin glass is their transparent smile
Over thin lips: the glass is dashed down suddenly
And murder glares. Their right hands hold
Their right hands, but the dangerous left
Fingers an invisible revolver. These men, we trust.
The cardinal cheers us with a dash of scarlet.
Bomb bomb bomb trumpets drums flutes
Oh lamb of God spare us
Aeroplanes tanks gas battleships
Bursting waves oh lamb of God
Pity us.
            'This modern Vienna
Is not incorruptible Athens witnessed by ageless suns,
But has survival controlled by thought
Is coloured by the long look of a searchlight.
Therefore therefore the moulding of History
Invests truth. Murder is necessary.
A scalpel excellently reduces

Warts, rebels. Even miracles
Have been performed, as the elimination of voices
That contradict official faces.
Or voices have been transplanted, and who
Once was our enemy, ripe and unseen,
Fearless as love, is now as true
As a dead voice played through on a machine.
Confession by torture. Also reproduced printed words
Of million newspapers, can change the idea of houses
As they alter the time of trains, doubt carbon manganese
    girders
In seeming New York. We say Vienna
Tenements were a fortress built by the workers
So we killed the workers to save the workers –
And when those houses were put up we said
The building materials used by the socialist municipality are of
    such inferior quality that the new working class tenements
    will soon fall to pieces.'

    If only one can silence every voice,
Assertion of the primitive crocus,
Flooded with snow, but melting not to water,
Melting into summer.

We listen at the walls of wombs. Does life
Contradict us? Life? Life? In oil-tarred pissoirs
(Odourless) amongst cartoons? In back streets,
In rooms with bugs, in courts with sunless flowers
Where radio crazily jazzes
And the gross arms of women beat their carpets?

Why did one dying, among their wounded,
In a dark groaning attic, suddenly sing?
And there moved as actively as on a movie screen
Before their eyes the May Day celebrating;

Memory of sky as blue as woman's veins
But with veins of red, sky blue and yellow

Rejoicing with them, and the blood flags streaming,
The crass grass for lovers' pillow.
They believe this will come again tomorrow.
It is their solid brain. The present, pictures.
Deny, deny, as dream their shelled houses.
Revenge is theirs. To us, sorrow.

Faces of our men beneath steel helmets
Should echo one face, stone face of a palace,
North Ocean reflecting vast speechless
Aims of ice stabbed in its depths.
Should have one face not many facets like water's
Broken surface splintering into
A hundred separations. An army should be
Weak with strength, exhausted with
Performing loads they raise that also
Nail them. Should be a giant tired
Between whose strength and thought clangs sleep.
But these, these reptile
Faces (so-called) utter a positive weakness,
The sulky heifer, the furnished goat, the
Famished blonde, the conscious good.
What is wrong?

The Stranger:

                    Supposing a stranger
One totally disinterested, not a sucker
Of his mother's milk from nipple of a shell
Soon to destroy him – his arterial circulation
Not a modern currency corrupted by inflation –
Should stand within northern range of us
Not staring frosty cracks such as
'Why does Dollfuss smile when he walks through the grass?
Because he's so short the blades tickle his arse.'
– A stranger's sandalled feet from cool hills

With just ankles and watching sense aware,
Listening to the flag that somewhat too loudly taps
Its wan mast; to the irregular brittle shocks
Of loyal volleys that seem perhaps
The whip and tramp of an approaching anger:
A stranger, a witness free from danger, observing
The lying snakes, the favourites of the sun
Those twisting ministers, infest a land
Where all the twigs seem snakes, and where all pops
The backfire of a car, a tactless cough
From traitor Fey, seem bombs; watching
The squall of fear an instant catch
A thousand faces, like the death sphinx paw
Murmuring on million desert: a stranger answering
What is wrong?
                           Fear, fear in armies
Breeds death.
                    Would he forgive us?
                                               Would he
Glance at a minister who smiles and smiles
'How now! A rat? Dead for a ducat.' Shoot!

III The Death of Heroes

Lucky: those who were shot dead:–
Outright not being and not being those
Thrown down cellar and trampled with nailed boots;
Made to swallow the badge with three arrows
That excellently deflect harmless into
A ground pegged out for making decent houses;
Beaten to death; left frozen
In the so gentle snow breeding all iron
Solid with their clenched rifles; or hanged
By an ignoring justice, fit only for colonies.

Our fatal unconfidence attempted a bridge
Between revolution and the already providing
World. Children, we said, must be filled
So the strike failed. Some men, the bravest
Fought at night and sullen flung down
Their hollow rifles, going to work at dawn.

Also, failure of leaders who betrayed us.
Of messengers silenced before the signal of
Danger: passage given to AUNT EMMA IS SICK
Meaning *Do Nothing*: arrest of those bearing
KARL IS SICK, meaning *Begin*.

First, when the lights failed, our spirit flared up
As a match spirts: then, when they took over the power station
And lights glared, trams budged: our match went out.
Their green signals for lights sliding their troop trains
And guns to smooth our death; their newspapers
With lying words foreknowingly cast in lead
By our fellow workers saying 'All but a small clique have fled'
And 'the red filth is bled': these things chiefly destroyed us.
Their foursquare voice through unassailable air
Proved that at no time were their brain tracks severed
Never their fingers in uncontrollable darkness fluttered.

Now we recollect, as an old one saying
'I was too old to fight, I write anonymously
You will know why. I lived with my son and wife
In the Goethe Hof. On that morning
Feb 13, I was pacing my white, loved room
My own, with windows on both sides, high up, like a tower,
Shedding enlightenment on our hands, the sign of power
(But there was no power); I paced and watched the court
With the blacklegs leaving for work. Our comrades
Blackly sulked back, watching. The blacklegs jeered
But in their hearts I have reason to believe that even the worst
    cheered.

At 10 a.m. the roaring shadow of a police aeroplane
Crossed the court. I crossed to my window on the street
And saw soldiers, who fired. From other windows we fired
   down.
I turned and spoke to my son. He said "Listen,
The howitzers begin". "Ha! That is Fey's joke
Making his big thud into February
When the ice echoes so." It was no joke to hear
And see my son lie dead. That was at 12.
There were four more whose dying choked the stairs.'

(After, he remembers that he helped.)

Those at Floridsdorf who bombarded the police station; the
   firemen who fought, led by Weissel; smuggling of guns
   and food to our comrades through the sewers; there
   was fighting underground; also on the pitchy bank of the
   canal.
   Those who tied sickle and hammer to a chimney flue; under
   the waving flag lay a child shot dead by the police: a mother
   and baby murdered in the Karl Marx Hof, which held out
   longest.
   Against this, at Meidling our leader refused to serve out
   arms: 'I refuse to send men to the slaughter house.' Other
   leaders were cowards. At Schlinger Hof, the police drove out
   all the women and children in front of the building, and
   threatened to fire on them. The workers surrendered.

There were some suffered from the destruction of houses
More than from death of men: they weep for their houses
That endured enormous wounds, a man's abyss.
So the once sun-flaked walls, our elaborated pride,
Were more our life than any man's one life, though proud.
Heroes are instantly replaced: civilization
Wears concrete sides: destroy these walls
With shell-holes, and our children wear their weals.

There are some flowers spring in our memory
There are some birds that cut the bare sky.
We in prison meditate much on the rare gentian,
Are terrible in our envy of the beasts' freedom,
Become dangerous as birds, as flowers. The dead, as stones.
Rosa Luxemburg wished finally to be a bird,
Watched grass and dreamt of orchids. Uttermost life is birds
Or undying anemone, as the dying man saying
'Here the insurrection ends, here revolution begins',
His saying this, not dying. Also, amongst those
The sulky heifer, the furnished goat, Fey's swine,
Who dared not even shoot, whose 'special tasks'
Were hanging, finishing off the wounded, insulting
The corpses in the street with placards
'Here lies the handwork of your leaders' –
One of Fey's boys left them and shouted 'For two years
I forsook the workers to kill the workers because
I was fed by these traitors. Now kill me.'
And an old man, one who had lost his son,
Embraced him 'Here is a rifle, you know whom to shoot.'

Fading, fading. On Wednesday, snow muffling
Our resistance. There were those escaping
Over the mountain bone white desert and falling
Dust, our land. Like stains of ink on satin
Is blood spreading in snow – the joy of huntin',
Their best since years. Life seems black against the snow.
To pick men with a gun is delicate
As pointing cleanest crochet. The vivid runner falls
From his hare-breathed anxiety: his undisputing
Hold on terror. O gently, whitely buried.
Less lucky those who hid in leafless woods
And caves of towns, their high-priced starving
Hunted as preciously as jewelled tiger
Amongst Indian boughs. Less lucky too
Those who ran far like images of winds

As cold as knives, eyeless and voiceless: heard
Incredible flames, the sound of welcome: had
Collapsing, reached the frontier. They related
How they had lost. The desolate
Praise mocks the defeated 'You're heroes'.

   Wallisch was on the mountains: climbed
With wife at side and followed by 400,
Carrying munitions and no provisions. Like diving monoplanes
Through precipice of air on polished metal,
Curled down on them the ski-troops. They sniped
And were repulsed. Through snowdrifts men dragged guns.
Like air-raid with naked flashes, thunder,
Collapsed the storm. They withstood it.
Fiercer than ice-blankets, more bitter than rifles' clicks,
Night brought a messenger with news of total loss.
Wallisch said 'Escape, and leave me.' The loved, brave man
And his wife left, alone. Descended at last.
Reached a waiting lorry. Started to Jugo Slavia.
The whole of Styria knew Wallisch; a worker watched,
Whose love dreamed on lotteries, and a safe state ticket
Drove up – the hunted leader. He won it. This man
Buried his money: blabbed: was found dead 10 days after.

Wallisch comforted his wife, who wept. In the court room
He spoke 'These murders lie on Fey
Who boasted of his clean-up. For many months
They have dispersed our societies, driven our meetings
Beneath the recognizing light. What we made almost free
Rent, rates, gas, the price of electricity,
They loaded with taxes, then publicly blamed us
And at the same time banned our defensive newspapers.
Our too-peace-offering unsinister organization
They rivalled with warlike and sinister organization.
What we inevitably have been, our inescapable defiant past,
Nobly weaponed, they made illegal. Searched our houses
Arrested our leaders, provoked our simpletons,

Signed sham concessions. Drove their legality
Against our establishment. We compromised
Too long. Our patience our defect.
                                    Now, I promised
My lads to help them when they needed help. This was my life.

'At the age of 11 I became a mason's apprentice
I was exploited even as a child.
At 16 I became an assistant and at 17
I made my travels in Austria and Germany
And saw oppression of the workers.
From 1914 to 1917 I fought in the War
And gained some distinction. I have been a socialist
Since 1905. I have only been a socialist.

'I have devoted my whole life to the workers
To serve their cause. I have enemies only
Because I fought for the workers so faithfully,
One must be ready to do all,
Ready to sacrifice oneself, even to lay down one's life.'

The square windows of the prison square surround him
    dumbly
Where a ditch was dug by criminals and a gallows set
And sand sprinkled. Then 56 soldiers
Armed to the teeth looked rather ridiculous
To guard 1 man. But we were watching
From all our cells, prison cells, cells of labour,
Our leader. They brought him out in a hurry
For Dollfuss had phoned through to complain of the delay;
Dollfuss, Dollfuss said 'Hang him low'.
Wallisch stood on the platform and before he died
'Live Socialism', and 'Hail Freedom', he said.
The word 'Freedom' was choked by the rope.

After, Wallisch was a word buried
In unmarked ground: but walls have ears and mouths

That uttered us his grave. At night for all their graves
We brought easy flowers in crude wreaths
Daisies, nasturtium, cornflower, sorrell, dandelion.
For the sick man hanged when he was too ill to stand up
For the one they brought to the hospital but the doctor said
'We have no beds unoccupied', and they took the hint
For unrecognizable swollen corpses found
Thrown in the river, not dead because they were drowned,
For those in hiding whom their women betrayed
By a difficult jealousy; poppy, geranium, wall-flower
Not involved orchid hypocrite politic lily
To remind them of what they were weary. We built
Upon their earth the wave of a new world
From flowers: each morning when light spelled
Its crested certainty, the police, afraid of daisies
Trampled the flowers. There was one who found
A bitter laurel branch: this one grabbed a bomb
– Blew off both hands. They were our little message
To grinning Fey, and Dollfuss being reported
'This is the saddest day in all my life'
To the cardinal cheering us with a spot of scarlet
Bomb, bomb, bomb, trumpets, drums, flutes!

Lucky, those who were killed outright: unlucky those
Burrowing survivors without 'tasks fit for heroes':
Constructing cells, ignorant of their leaders, assuming roles;
They change death's signal honour for a life of moles.

IV Analysis and Statement

Fading fading the importance
Of what was said
                    by so many voices
Between the sunset and the coffee;
So many faces, so many invitations.

Five Voices

A: 'Amongst friends, and therefore very alone,
Our understanding is a recognizable saviour
For ever a vision, beneath wounds, also beneath
Our least excusable behaviour.'

B: 'The immeasurable eye an instant wide
That feeds on fields of white and separates
The countless dark: I value its
Album of snaps.'

C: 'I love a friend
Who is external: to him the sky is brass,
Solid the grass where his behaving runs.
At night he sleeps well with limpid hands silent,
His character rings like the single stroke of a bell.
Loving, I've struck and struck upon this bell
Until at last I have become
A singular phantom
That haunts his constant dream.'

D: 'It is not what they stole nor what they spoiled
For they have their naked virtue, though far from me,
Real friendship and their own code for each other
(In a small sealed world and casual like brothers),
It is that my devotion they have spilled
And bled my veins of trust across their sport.

'There is no question more of not forgiving,
Forgiveness become my only feeling,
To understand their lack of understanding
Has absorbed my entire loving,
Yet sometimes I wish that I were loud and angry
Without this human mind like a doomed sky
That loves, as it must enclose, all.

'Later, doubtless, they will pause
In the midst of those gestures that so weave their world,

The little thefts, the charming lies, the smiles,
For my acts are explicit, and they will wonder
At images left and so completely willed.
These will disturb like a minor illness;
They will recall me as Unhappiness.'

E: 'At last we count only on corruption,
That men live from admiration;
That sincere death to them is what their glass
Only throwing back their image, says.
Their happiness itself becomes a trick.'

Whether the man living or the man dying
Whether this man's dead life, or that man's life dying . . .

A bronzed physical surface pleasing the eye
Boy's diving form that draws the day's whole eye
Is confused – by some obscenity
Of what the mind admires –
With the body's desire.

Beneath the lower ribs and the navel
I hold the desert, dividing my health
With five voices. As I grow older
Imaging the sands' outward empty form
My journeys grow wider,
Nearer and nearer to Africa.

I, I, I.

I think often of a woman
With dark eyes neglected, a demanding turn of the head
And hair of black silky beasts.
How admirable it is
They offer a surface bright as fruit in rain
That feeds on kissing. Loving is their conqueror
That turns all sunshine, fructifying lemons.
Our sexes are the valid flowers
Sprinkled across the total world and wet

With night. It surely was my father
His dry love his dry falling
Through dust and death to stamp my feature
That made me ever fear that fortunate posture.

Not love, not death, not the dead living;
Supposing a stranger.

Across the sliding tracks of shale
And through the fossiled ribs of a gaunt valley
To a pass where the cars make their crossing
I continued my travels through an unknown, mental country.
The bare slopes presupposed despair
Reminding me of cloths drawn over a hearse
And I looked for comfort to the freezing air.

Supposing a stranger.

In the middle of reading, or walking on the town pavement,
Or through the smoke of afternoon talk, I would strain my
    sense
To imagine what rocks against the sky
Surmounted a new range, like guns pointed in defence.

The live ones are . . .
I reached the ambition to despair.
Ignorant of history, all the day
Traffic shivered my bones like a malaria.
Time seemed foreshortened and confused with change
Not seen, monstrous with slowness like the Himalayan range.

But a stranger, not repeating the familiar curse
On traffic: curse that reasonably comforts. That at cross roads
Or in the stratosphere, progress smashes, fulfilling nightmares.
That final war cuts off the hydra heads
Of our young nations: the classics sigh, stir in contented
    chairs.
That these wicked, smiling ways of commerce
Like a late epoch in sculpture, so smoothed all over

And done in alabaster, drown in their own womanish tears.
He not soothing us with doom. Nor blessing
Like Love, his saints. Those who hang about
At jaws of lavatories, advertising their want of love,
Pilloried by their open failure: whose eyes are still innocent,
Confessing a real disappointment. Those who go to islands,
Whose salvaged happiness can greet their friends,
A few worthy of jokes. Those who sell all,
Give to their first prostitute: or buy the most flashing
Racing car or aeroplane: they dangle their jewelled contempt.
Those who fragilely repeat all sins: secure
Roman damnation: write diaries. Those with special grace
To prop up dahlias, to create tasks for the hopeless.
Theirs the singular climbing gaze of one calm when drowning.
Assurance and laughter are rare, they are dredged from the sea,
Vases dug from the graves of a gay, obliterated people,
Liars and buggers under the dark lid of centuries.
Not, not, not; but
Witnessing whole Europe as large as Greece to Athens,
Outside their stalking inner worlds, the dead man's life,
The real life a fading light the real death a light growing;
Berlin, Paris, London, this Vienna, emerging upon
Further terrible ghosts from dreams. He greets the
Historians of the future, the allies of no city,
O man and woman minute beneath their larger day;
Those burrowing beneath frontier, shot as spies because
Sensitive to new contours; those building insect cells
Beneath the monstrous shell of ruins; altering
The conformation of masses, that at last conjoin
Accomplished in justice to reject a husk.
Their walls already rest upon their dead, on Wallisch
Trapped in the mountains, on Weissel the engineer
Who lied to save his followers 'I forced them after
With my revolver'. On all the others. These are
Our ancestors.

1936–1938

The Half of Life

From the German of Hölderlin

Hang with yellow pears
And full with wild roses
The land in the lake,
You holy swans,
And drunk with kisses
Steep your heads
In sober and pious water.

Alas, where do I take, when
It is winter, the flowers, and where
The sunshine
And shadows of the earth?
The walls stand
Speechless and cold, in the wind
Clatter the flags.

[1936]

Buonaparte

From the German of Hölderlin

Holy vessels are the poets,
Wherein the wine of life, the spirit
Of heroes itself preserves.
But the spirit of this stripling
The swift one, must he not shatter,
Where it would comprehend him, the vessel?
The poet must leave him unattempted, as nature's ghost,
Before such matter the master becomes as a child.
Shall he live and remain in poetry?
No, he lives and remains in the world!

[1936]

The Town Shore at Barcelona

I walk down to the wind-swept winter shore
Where knifed-off slum blocks like stub teeth
With gaps and cheap enamel, post around
The blank and roaring mouth of sand.
This bony, falling jaw reads ocean's long advertisement
Endless with ozone and salts of disinfectant.

To my right, the cranes, poised birds
Coiled on their iron stilts admire the liner
Whose flamingo funnels and creamed, folded sides
Cliffed above nodding fields of handkerchiefs
Point to excitement of that glossing coast
Beyond me and the gasworks, where the clouds
Flaglike wave over mountain elephant hides.

Fixed in this central sand, bodies are derelict
Spoked wheels dismantled; minds are slag;
To the political eye men stink on scrap-heap;
But being less sensible than rusted machines
To know when they are waste, these cry with calls
Of cormorant, feed like gulls, and turn cartwheels;
Gentlemen lean and look from balustrades.

Paused in that dead town mouth, I note what winds
Have tanned the wrestlers redder than their sands
– Them waves applaud, for them foam thoughtless flowers.
Straddled against the sea, two gods contesting
Are mocked at by their sprawling girl whose breasts
Figure above the wet and dipping light
Like those of Ceres above her corn and horn.

Man passing, hiccups. I rattle trousered coins
And think how money, governmentally outlaid,
Could root these houses out. Imagine a boulevard
With sand-flowers bedded. Let palm-trees flourish

Their summer brocade and trumpet of success.
Race with your eyes the sport car boys and girls
Curvetting passionate tarmac coastal roads.

O the lights at night when horizontal syllables
From wave, hushed bush, and chinking cactus, lip;
The gramophones from off-shore insect boats;
Cicadas shrill in grass; red-hot guitars;
Bouquets from nightingales. Again, our lights
Endlessly repeated in electric stars.

But such is not. Rocket me in a lift
Of girdered skeleton towering from the dock
There where the aerial cable railway climbs
Till Barcelona withers to its map.
Drive me in trams down all main avenues.
Launch me as Icarus from this shore, whom winds
Eddy across the ocean in one gust.

What rimmed horizon like a noting sun
Tainted with Europe and the derelict coast
Has seared my path ascendant and melts down
Spirit-exalting wax to falling water?
Relapsed in the town jaws, I am a tongue
That praised the journeys of the mind
Coloured the sight, sang what it heard. All lies,
But the bone prison where I wag and mourn.

[1936]

Speech from a Play

Possibility, possibility of happiness
If I might restore
To unquiet Europe at least the evening peace
That mantles villages: one by one
The lights appear in the numbed valley

When the sun drops down: the hand falls
From plough or hammer: human work
Like stoops of crops
Under winter roof, is garnered away.
Stars' benediction remains, and above the turf
Hill, the unique pointing spire
Pins all the peace of sky to earth
As an assuaging cloak. And if
The hammer-headed cloud should threaten
Above the houses
Huddled like staring eyes of frightened life,
It is not we, but panic's self
Destroyed in tears upon us.

   [1936]

'If it were not too late!'

If it were not too late!
If I could mould my thought
To the curved form of that woman
With gleaming eyes, raven hair,
Lips drawn too tight like a scar,
Eye sockets shadowed with migraine's
Memory of earlier loves and wars
And her smile learnéd with being so human.

I imagined her lying naked at night
In warm rain when the breasts are watered
Through darkness by reflecting drops of light,
Which secret light accumulates
In pools on the skin as though on fruit.

Then her light blue dress she unloosed
Till light rose in rose and blue above the trees
Not to expel sad dreams, but to shine
On flesh that overflowed my eyes,

On life locking the senses with closeness,
O dawn of all my certainties!

If it were not too late.
If I could still concentrate
To clench my mind into a husk for love
I'd be too hot and ripe for ghosts,
Winds down side walks with swords of ice,
All betraying lies and lights.

For everything but she leads away
By brambles and along mechanic lines
To the suffering figures under trees
Of heroes who have wrecked happiness
And whose love is accomplished alone
In a spasm on the outer surface of the brain.

[1936]

Two Speeches from a Play

I

Civilization which was sweet
With love and words, after earthquakes
Terrifies; architraves
Or flowering leaf of the Corinthian capitol
Momently threaten; then fall
In marble waves on life. What was
The fastened mouth of the live past
Speaking in stone against the cloud, becomes
Our present death. O you
Whose thought – pathic through fear and greed –
Has frozen to that brittle shape
Dictated by what's actual in the world,
Which now breaks over us in all-destroying
Crash of injustice, know that your mental images

Are wailings of the falling cities
And photographs of battlefields. But you
Who still will live, dispart
The spiritual will from the material
Ruling pattern of rigid memory
And the system that haunts, to hew what's solid
After the living thought, not think what the dead have willed.
The mountain streams that have electric roots,
The stones
And metals, all of them our plant:
We'll tear from where they stick in minds
Now their possessors; give them as a prize
To those who've worked in fields and factories
For many centuries.
Into the image of a heart
That feeds separate functions with blood they need
For what they make, we'll shape the wealth
Of the dispossessed world and let those riches pour
Their fertilizing river delta
Across the starved sand of the peoples.
Fall marble, fall decay: but rise
Will of life in brothers: build
Stones in the form of justice: not justice
Into the fall of funeral monuments.

II

Is the eye heroic,
Lying soft in the face as reed-fringed pool,
Because for perceiving it looks to light
And rejects shadowy obstacles
And cuts through night like a diamond to the moon.
And has patience to stare a million years
Back to the sun clocked in primitive time?
Or is the mind heroic
Being boxed all life in prisoning skulls,

Lurking like a spy remote in the brain beyond dissection,
Because it has travelled further north than explorers
And does not freeze in interstellar space?
Eye sees what it sees, the mind
Knows what it must know.
Do not say I was a hero.
I used merely my eyes, I perceived
With my mind, my deeds sprang
From the sensible will.

[1937]

Ultimate Death

From the Spanish of Manuel Altolaguirre

Ultimate death: peace.
I know not whether to sing life
or mourn death.

Sailor, sailor,
you were the river, now are the sea.
I know not on what note to sing
in order to be more truthful,
for if from the compass of your death
peace was born, then stronger
than my grief should be my joy.

Ultimate death: peace.
I know not whether to sing your death
or mourn my life.

[1937]

My Brother Luis

From the Spanish of Manuel Altolaguirre

My brother Luis
used to kiss me doubting
on the platforms of the stations.
He always waited for me
or accompanied me to say goodbye
and now
when he left me to go I know not where
I did not arrive in time,
there was no one . . .
Not even the most remote echo
not even a shadow,
nor my reflection on the white clouds.
This sky is too immense.
Where are the sons of my brother?
Why are they not here?
I would go with them
amongst real things.
Perhaps they would give me his portrait.
I don't want them to be in a room
with black clothes.
It would be better if they ran by the river,
if they ran among flowers without looking at them,
like flowers also,
like boys,
who never stop,
as I have stopped,
too much at the edge of the sea and of death.

[1937]

In No Man's Land

Only the world changes, and time its tense
Against the creeping inches of whose moons
He launches his rigid continual present.

The grass will grow its summer beard and beams
Of sunlight melt the iron slumber
Where soldiers lie locked in their final dreams.

His corpse be covered with the white December
And roots push through his skin as through a drum
When the years and fields forget, but the bones remember.

[1938]

Concerning the Label Emigrant

From the German of Bertolt Brecht

I always found the name false which they gave us: Emigrants.
That means those who leave their country. But we
did not leave, of our own free will
choosing another land. Nor did we enter
into a land, to stay there, where possible forever.
Merely, we fled. We are driven out, banned.
Not a home, but an exile, is the land that took us in.
Restlessly we wait thus, as near as we can to the frontier
awaiting the day of return, every smallest alteration
observing beyond the boundary, zealously asking
every arrival, forgetting nothing and giving up nothing,
and also forgiving nothing which happened, forgiving nothing.
Ah, the silence of crimes does not deceive us! We hear the
    shrieks
from their camps even here. Yes, we ourselves
are almost like rumours of misdeeds, which escaped
over the frontier. Everyone of us

79

who with torn shoes walks through the crowd
bears witness of the scandal which now stains our land.
But none of us
will stay here. The final word
is yet unspoken.

[1938]

Hear This Voice

From the Spanish of Miguel Hernandez,
by Inez and Stephen Spender

Nations of the earth, fatherlands of the sea, brothers
of the world and of nothing:
inhabitants lost and more distant
from the sight than from the heart.

Here I have a voice impassioned,
here I have a life challenged and indignant,
here I have a message, here I have a life.

Look, I am opened, like a wound.
Look, I am drowned, drowned
in the midst of my people and its ills.
Wounded I go, wounded and badly wounded,
bleeding through the trenches and hospitals.

Men, worlds, nations,
pay heed, listen to my cry pouring out blood,
gather together the pulses of my breaking heart
into your spacious hearts,
because I clutch the soul when I sing.

Singing I defend myself
and I defend my people when the barbarians of crime
imprint on my people their hooves
of powder and desolation.

This is their work, this:
passing, they destroy like the whirlwind,
and before their funereal choler
the horizons are arms and the roads are death.

The lament pouring through valleys and balconies,
deluges the stones and works in the stones,
and there is no room for so much death
and there is no wood for so many coffins.

Caravans of beaten-down bodies.
All is bandages, pain and handkerchiefs:
all is stretchers on which the wounded
have broken their strength and their wings.

Blood, blood through the trees and the soil,
blood in the waters and on the walls,
and a fear that Spain will collapse
from the weight of the blood which soaks through her meshes
right to the bread which is eaten.

Gather together this gale,
nations, men, worlds,
which proceeds from the mouths of impassioned breath
and from hospitals of the dying.

Apply your ears
to my clamour of a violated people,
to the 'ay' of so many mothers, to the groans
of many a lucid being whom grief devoured.

The breasts which drove and wounded the mountains
see them languish without milk or beauty,
and see the white sweethearts and the black eyelashes
fallen and submissive in an obscure siesta.

Apply the passion of your entrails
to this people which dies with an invincible gesture
scattered by the lips and the brow,

beneath the implacable aeroplanes
which snatch terribly,
terribly ignominiously, every day,
sons from the hands of their mothers.

Cities of work and of innocence,
youths who blossom from the oak,
trunks of bronze, bodies of potency,
lie precipitated into ruin.

A future of dust advances,
a fate advances
in which nothing will remain:
nor stone on stone nor bone on bone.

Spain is not Spain, it is an immense trench,
a vast cemetery red and bombarded:
the barbarians have willed it thus.

The earth will be a dense heart, desolated,
if you, nations, men, worlds,
with the whole of my people,
and yours as well on their side,
do not break the ferocious fangs.

  [1938]

Madrid

From the Spanish of Manuel Altolaguirre

Horizon of war, whose lights,
whose unexpected sunrises, so brief,
whose fleeting dawns, promises, fires,
multiply the interminable death.
Here in Madrid, by night, solitary, sad,
the front and my frown are both synonymous
and above my gaze like a lament

the heroes crash, they fall submerged
in the green abyss of my face.
I know that I am deserted, that I am alone
that the front parallel with my frown,
disdains my grief and me accompanies.
Before the glorious circle of fire
I can evoke nothing, nor anything from anyone.
There is no memory, pleasure, lived before,
which I can call back from my past.
There is no absence, no legend, no hope
to calm my agony with its illusion.
Here in Madrid, facing death
my narrow heart keeps hidden
a love which grieves me which I cannot
even reveal to this night
before this immense field of heroism.

[1938]

The Word Dead and the Music Mad

The word on the hill
The music in the water –
The music reflects
The word on the guitar.

When the guns spoke
The fat poet fled
Till he came to Lerida,
Name peaceful as the dead.

The black spies watched
Trellised by balconies:
The poet hid in a cellar:
They reported to the police.

The police took down his name
And the words from his mouth

They found in his pockets
A letter from the South.

While the police read the letter
The poet stood silent
Staring at a dream
Of his childhood's violence.

He saw light flood a pillar
Stating summer's total sum:
A wolf leapt from behind it
And devoured a white lamb.

The ink on the paper
Seemed the wolf that tore
The white flesh of innocence
In a barbarous claw.

The black police seized his wrists
And tied them in fetters
They said 'A socialist,
Wrote you this letter.'

They drew their revolvers
And they shot him there
On a midsummer day
In peaceful Lerida.

The balconies clanged
Their bars like guitars
Where the spies and lies shone
Through a night of stars.

The police dissected
The tongues of peasants
To cut out the words
The poet had made pleasant.

A musician, friend
Of the poet, rose

His mind struck through
With one song to compose.

The musician stared
At the stillness of one word
The splitting moment
Of the single chord

When space divides
And the bullet flies
And, spun into terror,
Like worlds, float eyes.

The word was 'death'
And his mind froze
Fixed in the madness
Of terrible snows.

The word on the hill
The music in the water –
The music reflects
The word on the guitar.

[1938]

from TRIAL OF A JUDGE (1938)

ACT I

PETRA'S BROTHER: So far from gentle, he is the danger
His murderers and those who gave them orders
Still fear. They did not kill to kill
My already dying brother, stoned
By starvation, hunger heavier
Than a grave's alleviating weight of soil:
For visibly he belonged to dark
Death, like lean tendrils
Of sunless plants, prophesying shroud worms.

They shot only his face
That's still the face of what he is:
Their leaden bullets against a knife edge
Of steel, have tried to turn the blade:
But instantly when he died, the entire knife
Of what he thought and strove, glued to my hand.
He's dead. His living was one word
Influencing surrounding speech
Of a crowd's life, printless until
The words of all this time are frozen
By all our deaths into the winter library
Where life continually flows into books.
For us the blood still melts
We breathe a ripe or sparse or torturing air
And are the cursive act of history
Moving with fever, like distraction
In waves. I with dead sight
Of him you killed – with his undying will
Your bullets shot at – read
In your faces and your actions
Present history, and, in the reading, I shall write.
Myself a word amongst existing words
Reading your words, I see in them death's orders.
I tell you, this impartial judge
Weaker than his own justice, shall smile
And pardon Petra's murderers.
These prisoners, Petra's murderers,
Shall sit upon a bench to judge this judge;
And where my brother's life has printed
The contradiction to your world of lies
I'll stamp his truth again with my own breath,
Yes, even with my death.

ACT II

JUDGE: How strange it seems
That to me justice was once delineated by an inner eye

86

As sensibly as what is solid
In this room, tables, chairs and walls,
Is made indubitable by the sun.
But now all crumbles away
In coals of darkness, and the existence
Of what was black, white, evil, right
Becomes invisible, founders against us
Like lumber in a lightless garret.
I refresh myself in pleasant country
Or I stare round faces in a room
And although there is gold in the corn and gaiety
In a girl's eyes or sliding along the stream,
Everything is without a meaning.
Voices of hatred and of power
Call through my inner darkness
Only that might is right.

ACT III

FIANCÉE: When Petra slept with me,
I held the whole of life, but now that earth
With all its trees and lakes has turned away its side
And I am left in a cold space
Which is drained entirely of the two I love.
How can I work with friends or shoot my enemies,
Since if I measure population
Against these brothers, though they're dead, they live for me
More than the world and all survivors?
Your clever bullets which streamed through him
Put out the universe where it hung in his mind
And future time; for me who stay
Its comet lays waste forest tracks of meaning.
No remote caverns, untrodden spheres, delayed
Epochs, hold him where the heel may quicken
And our souls meet in music.
Throw down your revolvers. Your violence runs
Along rigid lines to destroy each other.

All we need is love. And yet we play
The meaningless game of a machine
Running in grooves laid down by death.
Go home and let me cry.

ACT IV

JUDGE: I speak from the centre of a stage
Not of a tragedy but a farce
Where I am the spiritual unsmiling clown
Defeated by the brutal swearing giant
Whose law is power, his order
Nature's intolerant chaos;
Here my defeat shows bare its desert
In which emptiness wins and force levels
Wastes meaningless except to mockery.
Laugh if you will at the mind's and body's weakness
Yet if you multiply my single death
By all the deaths for which it is one precedent,
You see in my fall the fall of cities,
In this my innocent injured protest,
The massacre of children; in the triumph
Of those who hold me here
Your history clamped in iron; your word ground
Beneath the oppression of an age of ice.

JUDGE: For by your law, the jungle
Is established; and the tiger's safety is guaranteed
When he hunts his innocent victim,
By all the iron of the police.
I condemned to death gunmen
And gangsters, but they are
The highest functions of this society;
Except perhaps for machine guns and those inhuman
Instruments of killing
Which are more powerful even than your fangs
Devoid of pity and the human spirit –

As indeed the time may show.
Where death is esteemed so highly,
Where death's administrators are the nation's ministers,
Here in death's court, judged by death's slaves,
I should be flattered to die: perhaps I am.
You could scarcely offer a more glittering honour.
I appeal to those
Who have sent the ambassadors of their powers
Into this room which well may be the tomb
Of justice for us and them
Not to conceal their horror
At the usurping of law by lawlessness
Itself made into law
To justify Petra's murder.
Let them speak as witnesses
That I am killed for nothing worse
Than my indignation against murderers,
My pity for those three who did no murder.
Let them note well my tragic error
Fatal to repeat
When I renounced my public anger
Before imagined expediency.
Then let them turn their faces to a future
Of solemn words broken by rule,
Of spiritual words burned up with libraries,
And the triumph of injustice;
Of tyrants who send their messages of terror
Against the civilized and helpless.
O let them witness
That my fate is the angel of their fate,
The angel of Europe,
And the spirit of Europe destroyed with my defeat.

ACT V

JUDGE: Dear friend, your world is the antipodes
Of the world of those

89

Who seal us in this living tomb:
And travelling there, where all seems opposite,
Yet all will be the same; only
Those who are now oppressed will be the oppressors,
The oppressors the oppressed. For your
World and theirs exist to maintain their worlds
And truth becomes the slave of the arrangements
Whilst abstract reasoning is treated as a traitor
Sniped at by necessity.

JUDGE: Yet I believe
That if we reject the violence
Which they use, we coil
At least within ourselves, that life
Which grows at last into a world.
Then, from the impregnable centre
Of what we are, we answer
Their injustice with justice, their running
Terroristic lie with fixed truth.
Our single and simple being
Will be the terrible angel
And white witness which though they deny
Betrays even their convoluted darkness.
But if we use their methods
Of lies and hate, then we betray
The achievement in ourselves; our truth
Becomes the prisoner of necessity
Equally with their untruth, ourselves
Their stone and stupid opposite.
And I believe
That in our acts we are responsible
Before a final judgment, whether indeed
Those legends of belief which made
The traditional sky fluid with prayer
Freeze time suddenly into a single crystal
Where history is transparent; or whether

Each generation is the outpost
Of a total spiritual territory
And defeats, even of necessity,
Are defeats indeed: for they transmit
The violence and hatred which we used
Into the children's faces which we breed
Until their faces become that single face
We gave our lives to kill.

THE STILL CENTRE (1939)

To Inez

PART ONE

Polar Exploration

Our single purpose was to walk through snow
With faces swung to their prodigious North
Like compass iron. As clerks in whited banks
With bird-claw pens column virgin paper,
To snow we added foot-prints.
Extensive whiteness drowned
All sense of space. We tramped through
Static, glaring days, Time's suspended blank.
That was in Spring and Autumn. Summer struck
Water over rocks, and half the world
Became a ship with a deep keel, the booming floes
And icebergs with their little birds:
Twittering Snow Bunting, Greenland Wheatear,
Red-throated Divers; imagine butterflies
Sulphurous cloudy yellow; glory of bees
That suck from saxifrage; crowberry,
Bilberry, cranberry, *Pyrola Uniflora*.
There followed Winter in a frozen hut
Warm enough at the kernel, but dare to sleep
With head against the wall – ice gummed my hair!
Hate Culver's loud breathing, despise Freeman's
Fidget for washing: love only the dogs
That whine for scraps, and scratch. Notice
How they run better (on short journeys) with a bitch.
In that, different from us.
Return, return, you warn. We do. There is
A network of railways, money, words, words, words.
Meals, papers, exchanges, debates,
Cinema, wireless: the worst, is Marriage.
We cannot sleep. At night we watch

A speaking clearness through cloudy paranoia.
These questions are white rifts:– Was
Ice our anger transformed? The raw, the motionless
Skies, were these the Spirit's hunger?
The continual and hypnotized march through snow,
The dropping nights of precious extinction, were these
Only the wide inventions of the will,
The frozen will's evasion? If this exists
In us as madness here, as coldness
In these summer, civilized sheets: Is the North,
Over there, a tangible, real madness,
A glittering simpleton, one without towns,
Only with bears and fish, a staring eye,
A new and singular sex?

Easter Monday

The corroded charred
Stems of iron town trees shoot pure jets
Of burning leaf. But the dust already
Quells their nervous flame: blowing from
The whitening spokes
Of wheels that flash away
And roar for Easter. The city is
A desert. Corinthian columns lie
Like chronicles of Kings felled on their sides
And the Acanthus leaf shoots other crowns
Of grass and moss. Sands and wires and glass
Glitter in empty, endless suns. . . . And
In the green meadows, girls in their first
Summer dresses, play. The hurdy-gurdy noise
Trumpets the valley, while egg-freckled arms
Weave their game. Children gather
Pap-smelling cowslips. Papers
Weightless as clouds, browse on the hills.

The bourgeois in tweeds
Holds in his golden spectacles'
Twin lenses, the velvet and far
Mountains. But look, rough hands
From trams, 'buses, bicycles, and of tramps,
Like one hand red with labour, grasp
The furred and future bloom
Of their falling, falling world.

Experience

What the eye delights in, no longer dictates
My greed to enjoy: boys, grass, the fenced-off deer.
It leaves those figures that distantly play
On the horizon's rim: they sign their peace, in games.
What is put away, stays removed: music which taps
The soft drums of the ear, I do not sleep with
Though whispering through my blood. Why should faces I
   pass,
Lights under evening trees, bewilder the breath
Which is a noteless, perpetual engine? Make mind reconsider
Projects?

There was a wood,
Habitation of foxes and fleshy burrows,
Where I learnt to uncast my childhood, and not alone,
I learnt, not alone. There were four hands, four eyes,
A third mouth of the dark to kiss. Two people
And a third not either: and both double, yet different.
I entered with myself. I left with a woman.

Good-bye now, good-bye: to the early and sad hills
Dazed with their houses, like a faint migraine.
Orchards bear memory in cloudy branches.
The entire world roared in a child's brain.
It suffers accidents. Now I am yours.

My questions only had their answer
When they were fully put.
    'There are two questioners, two answerers,
They must meet in a wood.'
The question, the answer
Were never yours or mine, but always, ours.

Exiles from Their Land, History Their Domicile

History has tongues
Has angels has guns – has saved has praised –
Today proclaims
Achievements of her exiles long returned
Now no more rootless, for whom her printed page
Glazes their bruised waste years in one
Balancing present sky.

See how her dead, like standards
Unfurled upon their shore, are cupped by waves:
The laurelled exiles, kneeling to kiss these sands.

Number there freedom's friends. One who
Within the element of endless summer,
Like leaf in amber, petrified by light,
Studied the root of action. One in a garret
Read books as though he broke up flints. Some met
In back rooms with hot red plush hangings,
And all outside the snow of foreign tongues.
One, a poet, went babbling like a fountain
Through parks. All were jokes to children.
All had the pale unshaven stare of shuttered plants
Exposed to a too violent sun.

Now all these
Drink their just praise from cups of waves;
And the translucent magnifying lights
Purify the achievement of their lives

With human bodies as words in history
Penned by their wills.

Their deeds and deaths are birds. They stop the invisible
Speed of our vacant sight across the sky.
In the past-coloured pigment of the mind's eye
They feed and fly and dwell.

Their time and land are death, since all
States and stays and makes
Them one with what they willed. We, who are living, seem
Exiles from them, more living: for we endure
Perpetual winter, waiting
Spring that will break our hardness into flowers
To set against their just and summer skies.

Our bodies are the pig and molten metal
Which theirs were once, before death cast
Their wills into those signatory moulds . . .

Yet in the fluid past simplicity
Of those who now return
To greet us and advise us and to warn
Not giving us their love, but as examples,
Where do we recognize
Their similarity
To our own wandering present uncertainty?

What miracle divides
Our purpose from our weakness? What selects
Our waking from our sleeping and our acts
From madness? Who recognizes
Our image by the head and balanced eyes
And forming hands, and not the hidden shames?
Who carves
Our will and day and acts as history
And our likeness into statues
That walk in groves with those who went before?

How are we justified?

O utter with your tongues
Of angels, fire your guns – O save and praise –
Recall me from life's exile, let me join
Those who now kneel to kiss their sands,
And let my words restore
Their printed, laurelled, victoried message.

The Past Values

Alas for the sad standards
In the eyes of the old masters
Sprouting through glaze of their pictures!

For what we stare at through glass
Opens on to our running time:
As nature spilled before the summer mansion
Pours through windows in on our dimension.

And the propeller's rigid transparent flicker
To airman over continental ranges
Between him and the towns and river
Spells dynamics of this rotating
Age of invention, too rapid for sight.

Varnish over paint and dust across glass:
Stare back, remote, the static drum;
The locked ripeness of the Centaurs' feast;
The blowing flags, frozen stiff
In a cracked fog, and the facing
Reproach of self-portraits.

Alas for the sad standards
In the eyes of the freshly dead young
Sprawled in the mud of battle.

Stare back, stare back, with dust over glazed
Eyes, their gaze at partridges,

Their dreams of girls, and their collected
Faith in home, wound up like a little watch.

To ram them outside time, violence
Of wills that ride the cresting day
Struck them with lead so swift
Their falling sight stared through its glass.
Our sight stares back on death, like glass
Infringing the rigid eyes with toneless glaze,
Sinking stretched bodies inch-deep in their frames.

Through glass their eyes meet ours
Like standards of the masters
That shock us with their peace.

An Elementary School Class Room in a Slum

Far far from gusty waves, these children's faces.
Like rootless weeds the torn hair round their paleness.
The tall girl with her weighed-down head. The paper-
seeming boy with rat's eyes. The stunted unlucky heir
Of twisted bones, reciting a father's gnarled disease,
His lesson from his desk. At back of the dim class,
One unnoted, sweet and young: his eyes live in a dream
Of squirrels' game, in tree room, other than this.

On sour cream walls, donations. Shakespeare's head
Cloudless at dawn, civilized dome riding all cities.
Belled, flowery, Tyrolese valley. Open-handed map
Awarding the world its world. And yet, for these
Children, these windows, not this world, are world,
Where all their future's painted with a fog,
A narrow street sealed in with a lead sky,
Far far from rivers, capes, and stars of words.

Surely Shakespeare is wicked, the map a bad example
With ships and sun and love tempting them to steal –
For lives that slyly turn in their cramped holes

From fog to endless night? On their slag heap, these children
Wear skins peeped through by bones and spectacles of steel
With mended glass, like bottle bits on stones.
All of their time and space are foggy slum
So blot their maps with slums as big as doom.

Unless, governor, teacher, inspector, visitor,
This map becomes their window and these windows
That open on their lives like crouching tombs
Break, O break open, till they break the town
And show the children to the fields and all their world
Azure on their sands, to let their tongues
Run naked into books, the white and green leaves open
The history theirs whose language is the sun.

The Uncreating Chaos

I

To the hanging despair of eyes in the street, offer
Your making hands and your guts on skewers of pity.
When the pyramid sky is piled with clouds of sand which the
    yellow
Sun blasts above, respond to that day's doom
With a headache. Let your ghost follow
The young men to the Pole, up Everest, to war: by love, be
    shot.

For the uncreating chaos descends
And claims you in marriage: though a man, you were ever a
    bride:
Ever beneath the supple surface of summer muscle,
The fountain evening talk cupping the summer stars,
The student who chucks back the lock from his hair in front of
    a silver glass,
You were only anxious that all these passions should last.

The engine in you, anxiety,
Was a grave lecher, a globe-trotter, one
Whose moods were straws, the winds that puffed them,
    aeroplanes.
'Whatever happens, I shall never be alone,
I shall always have an affair, a railway fare, or a revolution.'

Without your buttressing gesture that yet so leans;
Is glad as a mat
When stamped on; blood that gives suck to a vampire bat;
And your heart fretted by winds like rocks at Land's End:
You'd stand alone in a silence that never uttered
And stare in yourself as though on a desolate room.

II

I stand so close to you,
I will confess to you.
At night I'm flooded by a sense of future,
The bursting tide of an unharnessed power
Drowning the contours of the present.

In thoughts where pity is the same as cruelty,
Your life and mine seem water. Whether
What flows and wavers is myself
Or my thought streaming over you – or over all
The town and time – we are the same.

But beyond windows of this waking dream
Facts do their hundred miles an hour
Snorting in circles round the plain;
The bikes and track are real; and yet the riders lose
All sense of place; they're ridden by
Their speed; the men are the machines.

All I can warn you now – more I shall learn –
Is that our fear makes all its opposite.
Your peace bursts into war.

You're coined into a savage when you flee
The splitting crystal civilization dangles.
And when you choose a lover like a mirror
You see yourself reflected as a gunman.

You are a ghost amongst the flares of guns
Less living than
The shattered dead whose veins of mineral
We mine for here.
                    Alter your life.

   III

Dissection of Empires, multiplication of crowns
By secret Treaty. But the pigeons scatter
Above the pavement at the fatal shot.
Heads bounce down stone steps.

Meagre men shoot up. Rockets, rockets,
A corporal's fiery tongue wags above burning parliament.
There flows in the tide of killers, the whip-masters,
Breeches and gaiters camouflage blood.

O visions of a faltering will
Inventing violent patterns!

History rushes. The crowds in towns,
Cerebral boundaries of nations over mountains,
Actors in flesh and death and material nature,
Dance to a gripless private stammer of shouting
. . . Thoughts in a dying minister's brain.

   IV

Shall I never reach
The field guarded by stones
Precious in the stone mountains,
Where the scytheless wind
Flushes the warm grasses:

Where clouds without rain
Add to the sun
Their lucid sailing shine?
The simple mechanism is here,
Clear day, thoughts of the work-room, the desk,
The hand, symbols of power.
Here the veins may pour
Into the deed, as the field
Into the standing corn.
Meanwhile, where nothing's pious
And life no longer willed,
Nor the human will conscious,
Holy is lucidity
And the mind that dare explain.

PART TWO

Hölderlin's Old Age

When I was young I woke gladly in the morning
With the dew I grieved, towards the close of day.
Now, when I rise, I curse the white cascade
That refreshes all roots, and I wish my eyelids
Were dead shutters pushed down by the endless weight
Of a mineral world. How strange it is, that at evening
When prolonged shadows lie down like cut hay,
In my mad age I rejoice, and my soul sings,
Burning vividly in the centre of a cold sky.

Hampstead Autumn

In the fat autumn evening street
Hands from my childhood stretch out
And ring muffin bells. The Hampstead
Incandescence burns behind windows
With talk and gold warmth.
Those brothers who we were lie wrapped in flannel,
And how like a vase looks my time then
Rounded with meals laid on by servants
With reading alone in a high room and looking down on
The pleasures of the spoiled pets in the garden –
A vase now broken into fragments,
Little walks which quickly reach their ends,
The islands in the traffic. To questions – I know not what –
Answers hurry back from the world,
But now I reject them all.
I assemble an evening with space
Pinned above the four walls of the garden,
A glowing smell of being under canvas,

The sunset tall above the chimneys,
From behind the smoke-screen of poplar leaves
A piano cutting out its images,
Continuous and fragile as china.

In the Street

After the lies and lights of the complex street
Cat-calls of vice, virtue's conceit, I shall be glad to greet
A blank wall with my self face to face
And between the intricate stones no speaking lip of excuse.

The Room above the Square

The light in the window seemed perpetual
Where you stayed in the high room for me;
It flowered above the trees through leaves
Like my certainty.

The light is fallen and you are hidden
In sunbright peninsulas of the sword:
Torn like leaves through Europe is the peace
Which through me flowed.

Now I climb alone to the dark room
Which hangs above the square
Where among stones and roots the other
Peaceful lovers are.

The Marginal Field

On the chalk cliff edge struggles the final field
Of barley smutted with tares and marbled
With veins of rusted poppy as though the plough had bled.
The sun is drowned in bird-wailing mist,

The sea and sky meet outside distinction,
The landscape glares and stares – white poverty
Of gaslight diffused through frosted glass.

This field was the farmer's extremest thought
And its flinty heart became his heart
When he drove below the return it yields
The wage of the labourer sheeted in sweat.
Here the price and the cost cross on a chart
At a point fixed on the margin of profit
Which opens out in the golden fields

Waving their grasses and virile beards
On the laps of the dripping valleys and flushing
Their pulsing ears against negative skies.
Their roots clutch into the flesh of the soil,
As they fall to the scythe they whisper of excess
Heaped high above the flat wavering scale
Near the sea, beyond the wind-scarred hill

Where loss is exactly equalled by gain
And the roots and the sinews wrestle with stone
On the margin of what can just be done
To eat back from the land the man the land eats.
Starved outpost of wealth and final soldier,
Your stretched-out bones are the frontier of power
With your mouth wide open to drink in lead.

A Footnote

(from Marx's Chapter on The Working Day)

'Heard say that four times four is eight,'
'And the king is the man what has all the gold.'
'Our king is a queen and her son's a princess
And they live in a palace called London, I'm told.'

'Heard say that a man called God who's a dog
Made the world with us in it,' 'And then I've heard
There came a great flood and the world was all drownded
Except for one man, and he was a bird.'

'So perhaps all the people are dead, and we're birds
Shut in steel cages by the devil, who's good,
Like the miners in their pit cages
And us in our chimneys to climb, as we should.'

– Ah, twittering voices
Of children crawling on their knees
Through notes of Blue Books, History Books,
At foot of the most crowded pages,
You are the birds of a songless age
Young like the youngest gods, rewarded
With childhood that for ever stays.
Stunted spirits in a fog
Woven over the whole land
Into brown tapestries,
You cry among the wheels and endless days
To your stripped and holy mothers
With straps tied around their waists
For dragging trucks along a line.
In the sunset above these towns
Often I watch you lean upon the clouds
Momently drawn back like a curtain
Revealing a serene, waiting eye
Above a tragic, ignorant age.

Thoughts during an Air Raid

Of course, the entire effort is to put myself
Outside the ordinary range
Of what are called statistics. A hundred are killed
In the outer suburbs. Well, well, I carry on.

So long as the great 'I' is propped upon
This girdered bed which seems more like a hearse,
In the hotel bedroom with flowering wallpaper
Which rings in wreathes above, I can ignore
The pressure of those names under my fingers
Heavy and black as I rustle the paper,
The wireless wail in the lounge margin.
Yet supposing that a bomb should dive
Its nose right through this bed, with me upon it?
The thought is obscene. Still, there are many
To whom my death would only be a name,
One figure in a column. The essential is
That all the 'I's should remain separate
Propped up under flowers, and no one suffer
For his neighbour. Then horror is postponed
For everyone until it settles on him
And drags him to that incommunicable grief
Which is all mystery or nothing.

View from a Train

The face of the landscape is a mask
Of bone and iron lines where time
Has ploughed its character.
I look and look to read a sign,
Through errors of light and eyes of water
Beneath the land's will, of a fear
And the memory of chaos,
As man behind his mask still wears a child.

The Midlands Express

Muscular virtuoso!
Once again you take the centre of the stage,

The flat Midlands.
The signals are all down, the curtain is raised
As with unerring power you drive
Straight to your goal.
You pull down all the Northern iron-rifted
Mountains to your knees,
Until they're pressed beneath your feet
Dragging my sight back with their weight.
You drive the landscape like a herd of clouds
Moving against your horizontal tower
Of steadfast speed.
All England lies beneath you like a woman
With limbs ravished
By one glance carrying all these eyes.
O juggler of the wheeling towns and stars
Unpausing even with the night,
Beneath my lines I read your iron lines
Like the great art beneath a little life
Whose giant travelling ease
Is the vessel of its effort and fatigue.

The Indifferent One

I take the lift to the eighth floor,
Walk through the steam of corridors
And knock at the numbered door.
Entering the porch, I pass
My face reflected palely in a glass,
Lean, with hollows under the eyes,
A heightened expression of surprise,
Skin porous, like cells in a hive,
And I think: 'Can you forgive?'

Yes, you accept. On the thin bed
Above the city night we float

Embodied on the waves, their boats,
Arm locked in arm, head against head,
Whilst the nerves' implicit contacts
Through the hidden cables spark.
All dips and enters and forgets in dark
Except my single staring sight
Hanging above its pilot light.

Upturned to the unwritten ceiling
My eyes there read another you,
The naked human figure leaning
With one hand raised towards a view
Between whose hills are the blue spaces,
Perspectives of my happiness!
There on your lips the clear light lives
Diffusing with its equable waves
The smile's indifference which forgives.

Three Days

Our three long and spacious days
Rounded with their summer skies
Above the sea among
The islands of the hills, where, standing
Upon the morning's tufted height, we saw
Across the valleys of the afternoon, our distant
Goal of evening resting on a point
Stretched into the waves,
Are dropped like unknown lives in oceans
To complete their oblivion –
Spiral journeys to happiness made short
As a past or passing thought.

What can I do, now I return, to hold
Against the present their little memory?
From the rhythm of the country-drinking body

What muscle asserts happiness against
The anxiety of the city?
What words we spoke sustain their singing birds
Against the printed flood of words?
What peace we gave each other signs
Away the storm of wars?

There swims within my life a fish
Which is the deep and glittering wish
Evoking all the hills and waters
Of sensual memories.
Your image and those days of glass
Being lost become no loss
But change into that image
At the centre of my thought,
Itself no less precious
Than the original happiness.

PART THREE

Two Armies

Deep in the winter plain, two armies
Dig their machinery, to destroy each other.
Men freeze and hunger. No one is given leave
On either side, except the dead, and wounded.
These have their leave; while new battalions wait
On time at last to bring them violent peace.

All have become so nervous and so cold
That each man hates the cause and distant words
Which brought him here, more terribly than bullets.
Once a boy hummed a popular marching song,
Once a novice hand flapped the salute;
The voice was choked, the lifted hand fell,
Shot through the wrist by those of his own side.

From their numb harvest all would flee, except
For discipline drilled once in an iron school
Which holds them at the point of a revolver.
Yet when they sleep, the images of home
Ride wishing horses of escape
Which herd the plain in a mass unspoken poem.

Finally, they cease to hate: for although hate
Bursts from the air and whips the earth like hail
Or pours it up in fountains to marvel at,
And although hundreds fall, who can connect
The inexhaustible anger of the guns
With the dumb patience of these tormented animals?

Clean silence drops at night when a little walk
Divides the sleeping armies, each
Huddled in linen woven by remote hands.
When the machines are stilled, a common suffering

Whitens the air with breath and makes both one
As though these enemies slept in each other's arms.

Only the lucid friend to aerial raiders,
The brilliant pilot moon, stares down
Upon the plain she makes a shining bone
Cut by the shadow of many thousand bones.
Where amber clouds scatter on no-man's-land
She regards death and time throw up
The furious words and minerals which kill life.

Ultima Ratio Regum

The guns spell money's ultimate reason
In letters of lead on the spring hillside.
But the boy lying dead under the olive trees
Was too young and too silly
To have been notable to their important eye.
He was a better target for a kiss.

When he lived, tall factory hooters never summoned him.
Nor did restaurant plate-glass doors revolve to wave him in.
His name never appeared in the papers.
The world maintained its traditional wall
Round the dead with their gold sunk deep as a well,
Whilst his life, intangible as a Stock Exchange rumour, drifted
    outside.

O too lightly he threw down his cap
One day when the breeze threw petals from the trees.
The unflowering wall sprouted with guns,
Machine-gun anger quickly scythed the grasses;
Flags and leaves fell from hands and branches;
The tweed cap rotted in the nettles.

Consider his life which was valueless
In terms of employment, hotel ledgers, news files.

Consider. One bullet in ten thousand kills a man.
Ask. Was so much expenditure justified
On the death of one so young and so silly
Lying under the olive trees, O world, O death?

The Coward

Under the olive trees, from the ground
Grows this flower, which is a wound.
It is easier to ignore
Than the heroes' sunset fire
Of death plunged in their willed desire
Raging with flags on the world's shore.
Its opened petals have no name
Except the coward's nameless shame
Whose inexpiable blood
For his unhealing wound is food.
A man was killed, not like a soldier
With lead but with rings of terror;
To him, that instant was the birth
Of the final hidden truth
When the troopship at the quay,
The mother's care, the lover's kiss,
The following handkerchiefs of spray,
All led to the bullet and to this.
Flesh, bone, muscle and eyes
Assembled in a tower of lies
Were scattered on an icy breeze
When the deceiving past betrayed
All their perceptions in one instant,
And his true gaze, the sum of present,
Saw his guts lie beneath the trees.

Lest every eye should look and see
The answer to its life as he,

When the flesh prizes are all lost
In that white second of the ghost
Who grasps his world of loneliness
Sliding into empty space:
I gather all my life and pour
Out its love and comfort here.
To populate his loneliness,
And to bring his ghost release,
My love and pity shall not cease
For a lifetime at least.

A Stopwatch and an Ordnance Map

A stopwatch and an ordnance map.
At five a man fell to the ground
And the watch flew off his wrist
Like a moon struck from the earth
Marking a blank time that stares
On the tides of change beneath.
All under the olive trees.

A stopwatch and an ordnance map.
He stayed faithfully in that place
From his living comrade split
By dividers of the bullet
That opened wide the distances
Of his final loneliness.
All under the olive trees.

A stopwatch and an ordnance map.
And the bones are fixed at five
Under the moon's timelessness;
But another who lives on
Wears within his heart for ever
The space split open by the bullet.
All under the olive trees.

War Photograph

Where the sun strikes the rock and
The rock plants its shadowed foot
And the breeze distracts the grass and fern frond,

There, in the frond, the instant lurks
With its metal fang planned for my heart
When the finger tugs and the clock strikes.

I am that numeral which the sun regards,
The flat and severed second on which time looks,
My corpse a photograph taken by fate;

Where inch and instant cross, I shall remain
As faithful to the vanished moment's violence
As love fixed to one day in vain.

Only the world changes, and time its tense,
Against the creeping inches of whose moon
I launch my wooden continual present.

The grass will grow its summer beard and beams
Of light melt down the waxen slumber
Where soldiers lie dead in an iron dream;

My corpse be covered with the snows' December
And roots push through skin's silent drum
When the years and fields forget, but the whitened bones
    remember.

Sonnet

The world wears your image on the surface
And judges, as always, the looks and the behaviour
Moving upon the social glass of silver;
But I plunged through those mirrored rays
Where eye remarks eye from the outside,

Into your hidden inner self and bore
As my self-love your hopes and failure,
The other self for which my self would have died.

Drowned in your life, I there encountered death
Which claimed you for a greater history
Where the free win, though many win too late.
We being afraid, I made my hand a path
Into this separate peace which is no victory
Nor general peace, but our escape from fate.

Fall of a City

All the posters on the walls
All the leaflets in the streets
Are mutilated, destroyed or run in rain,
Their words blotted out with tears,
Skins peeling from their bodies
In the victorious hurricane.

All the names of heroes in the hall
Where the feet thundered and the bronze throats roared,
Fox and Lorca claimed as history on the walls,
Are now angrily deleted
Or to dust surrender their dust,
From golden praise excluded.

All the badges and salutes
Torn from lapels and from hands
Are thrown away with human sacks they wore,
Or in the deepest bed of mind
They are washed over with a smile
Which launches the victors when they win.

All the lessons learned, unlearnt;
The young, who learned to read, now blind
Their eyes with an archaic film;

The peasant relapses to a stumbling tune
Following the donkey's bray;
These only remember to forget.

But somewhere some word presses
On the high door of a skull, and in some corner
Of an irrefrangible eye
Some old man's memory jumps to a child
– Spark from the days of energy.
And the child hoards it like a bitter toy.

At Castellon

Backed to the brown walls of the square
The lightless lorry headlamps stare
With glinting reflectors through the night
At our gliding star of light.

Houses are tombs, tarpaulins cover
Mysterious trucks of the lorries over.
The town vacantly seems to wait
The explosion of a fate.

Our cigarettes and talking stir
Beneath the walls a small false ember.
A sentry stops us at his hut
Stamping with his rifle-butt.

Beside him stands a working man
With cheeks where suns have run.
'Take this comrade to the next village.'
The lines ploughed with ravage

Lift to a smile, the eyes gleam
And then relapse into their dream.
Head bent, he shuffles forward
And in without a word.

The car moves on to suns and time
Of safety for us and him.
But behind us on the road
The winged black roaring fates unload

Cargoes of iron and of fire
To delete with blood and ire
The will of those who dared to move
From the furrow, their life's groove.

The Bombed Happiness

Children, who extend their smile of crystal,
And their leaping gold embrace,
And wear their happiness as a frank jewel,
Are forced in the mould of the groaning bull
And engraved with lines on the face.

Their harlequin-striped flesh,
Their blood twisted in rivers of song,
Their flashing, trustful emptiness,
Are trampled by an outer heart that pressed
From the sky right through the coral breast
And kissed the heart and burst.

This timed, exploding heart that breaks
The loved and little hearts, is also one
Splintered through the lungs and wombs
And fragments of squares in the sun,
And crushing the floating, sleeping babe
Into a deeper sleep.

Its victoried drumming enters
Above the limbs of bombed laughter
The body of an expanding State
And throbs there and makes it great,
But nothing nothing can recall

Gaiety buried under these dead years,
Sweet jester and young playing fool
Whose toy was human happiness.

Port Bou

As a child holds a pet
Arms clutching but with hands that do not join
And the coiled animal watches the gap
To outer freedom in animal air,
So the earth-and-rock flesh arms of this harbour
Embrace but do not enclose the sea
Which, through a gap, vibrates to the open sea
Where ships and dolphins swim and above is the sun.
In the bright winter sunlight I sit on the stone parapet
Of a bridge; my circling arms rest on a newspaper
Empty in my mind as the glittering stone
Because I search for an image
And seeing an image I count out the coined words
To remember the childish headlands of this harbour.
A lorry halts beside me with creaking brakes
And I look up at warm waving flag-like faces
Of militiamen staring down at my French newspaper.
'How do they speak of our struggle, over the frontier?'
I hold out the paper, but they refuse,
They did not ask for anything so precious
But only for friendly words and to offer me cigarettes.
In their smiling faces the war finds peace, the famished mouths
Of the rusty carbines brush against their trousers,
Almost as fragilely as reeds;
And wrapped in a cloth – old mother in a shawl –
The terrible machine-gun rests.
They shout, salute back as the truck jerks forward
Over the vigorous hill, beyond the headland.
An old man passes, his running mouth,

With three teeth like bullets, spits out 'pom-pom-pom'.
The children run after; and, more slowly, the women,
Clutching their clothes, follow over the hill;
Till the village is empty, for the firing practice,
And I am left alone on the bridge at the exact centre
Where the cleaving river trickles like saliva.
At the exact centre, solitary as a target,
Where nothing moves against a background of cardboard
   houses
Except the disgraceful skirring dogs; and the firing begins,
Across the harbour mouth from headland to headland,
White flecks of foam gashed by lead in the sea;
And the echo trails over its iron lash
Whipping the flanks of the surrounding hills.
My circling arms rest on the newspaper,
My mind seems paper where dust and ink fall,
I tell myself the shooting is only for practice,
And my body seems a cloth which the machine-gun stitches
Like a sewing machine, neatly, with cotton from a reel;
And the solitary, irregular, thin 'paffs' from the carbines
Draw on long needles white threads through my navel.

PART FOUR

Darkness and Light

To break out of the chaos of my darkness
Into a lucid day is all my will.
My words like eyes in night, stare to reach
A centre for their light: and my acts thrown
To distant places by impatient violence
Yet lock together to mould a path of stone
Out of my darkness into a lucid day.

Yet, equally, to avoid that lucid day
And to preserve my darkness, is all my will.
My words like eyes that flinch from light, refuse
And shut upon obscurity; my acts
Cast to their opposites by impatient violence
Break up the sequent path; they fly
On a circumference to avoid the centre.

To break out of my darkness towards the centre
Illumines my own weakness, when I fail;
The iron arc of the avoiding journey
Curves back upon my weakness at the end;
Whether the faint light spark against my face
Or in the dark my sight hide from my sight,
Centre and circumference are both my weakness.

O strange identity of my will and weakness!
Terrible wave white with the seething word!
Terrible flight through the revolving darkness!
Dreaded light that hunts my profile!
Dreaded night covering me in fears!
My will behind my weakness silhouettes
My territories of fear, with a great sun.

I grow towards the acceptance of that sun
Which hews the day from night. The light
Runs from the dark, the dark from light
Towards a black or white of total emptiness.
The world, my body, binds the dark and light
Together, reconciles and separates
In lucid day the chaos of my darkness.

The Human Situation

This I is one of
The human machines
So common on the gray plains –
Yet being built into flesh
My single pair of eyes
Contain the universe they see;
Their mirrored multiplicity
Is packed into a hollow body
Where I reflect the many, in my one.

The traffic of the street
Roars through my head, as in the genitals
Their unborn London.

And if this I were destroyed,
The image shattered,
My perceived, rent world would fly
In an explosion of final judgement
To the ends of the sky,
The colour in the iris of the eye.

Opening, my eyes say 'Let there be light',
Closing, they shut me in a coffin.
To perform the humming of my day,
Like the world, I shut the other
Stars out from my sky.

All but one star, my sun,
My womanly companion,
Revolving round me with light
Eyes that shine upon my profile
While the other profile lies in night.

My body looms as near me as, to the world,
The world. Eyelashes
Are reeds fringing a pond
Which shut out the moon.
Ranges, vertebrae, hair, skin, seas.
Everything is itself, nothing a map.
What's inside my bowels and brain,
The Spring and the volcanoes,
Include all possibilities of development
Into an unpredictable future,
Full of invention, discovery, conversion, accident.

No one can track my past
On a chart of intersecting lines:
No fountain-pen is filled from the womb
As I from my mother's blood stream.
My history is my ancestry
Written in veins upon my body:
It is the childhood I forget
Spoken in words I mispronounce:
In a caligraphy of bones
I live out some hidden thought
Which my parents did forget.

Faces of others seem like stars
Obedient to symmetrical laws.
I stare at them as though into a glass,
And see the external face of glass,
My own staring mask of glass,
Tracked with lines of reflexes.
Eyes, lashes, lips, nostrils, brows.
The distant features move on wires

Fixed to their withheld characters.

O law-giving, white-bearded father,
O legendary heroes, sailing through dreams
Looking for land when all the world was sea
And sunrise, O bare-kneed captain of my first school,
O victors of history, angry or gentle exponents
Of the body as an instrument which cuts
A pattern on the time, O love
Surrounding my life with violet skies,

It is impossible for me to enter
The unattainable ease
Of him who is always right and my opponent,
Of those who climb the dawn with such flexible knees,
Of those who won the ideologic victories,
Of her whose easy loving turned to flowers
The forbidden and distorted natural powers;
Impossible to imagine, impossible to wish
The entrance into their symbolic being
Death to me and my way of perceiving
As much as if I became a stone;
Here I am forced on to my knees,
On to my real and own and only being
As into the fortress of my final weakness.

The Separation

When the night within whose deep
Our minds and bodies melt in love,
Instead of joining us, divides
With winds and seas that tear between
Our separated sleep –

Then to my lidless eyes that stare
Beyond my dark and climbing fears,
Your answering warm island lies

In the gilt wave of desire
Far as the day from here.

Here where I lie is the hot pit
Crowding on the mind with coal
And the will turned against it
Only drills new seams of darkness
Through the dark-surrounding whole.

Our vivid suns of happiness
Withered from summer, drop their flowers;
Hands of the longed, withheld tomorrow
Fold on the hands of yesterday
In double sorrow.

The present voices and the faces
Of strangers mirroring each other
In their foreign happiness,
Lay waste and populate my map
With meaningless names of places.

To bring me back to you, the earth
Must turn, the aeroplane
Must fly across the glittering spaces,
The clocks must run, the scenery change
From mountains into town.

Against a wheel I press my brain,
My blood roars through a night of wood
But my heart uncoils no shoot
From the centre of a silence
Of motionless violence.

And when we meet – the ribs will still
Divide the flesh-enfolding dream
And the winds and seas of time
Ruin the islands with their stream
However compassed be the will;

Unless within the turning night
Where we are ever separate,
Our eyes drink in each other's silence,
Unmeasuring patience
Threaded upon their secret light.

Shuttered by dark at the still centre
Of the world's circular terror,
O tender birth of life and mirror
Of lips, where love at last finds peace
Released from the will's error.

Two Kisses

I wear your kiss like a feather
Laid upon my cheek
And I wander to the quay where the river
Suggests suggests

The dirt off all the streets
And the rotting feet of factories,
But the swans and boats and corks ride
The buoyant running waters
And the eye is carried by a tide

To the far shore and day-green spaces,
And the ear is gently belied
By sounds under dreams under the roar outside.
And then the heart in its white sailing pride

Launches among the swans and the stretched lights
Laid on the water, as on your cheek
The other kiss and my listening
Life, waiting for all your life to speak.

The Little Coat

The little coat embroidered with birds
Is irretrievably ruined.
We bought it in the Spring
And she stood upon a chair,
A blazing tree of birds;
I leaned my head against her breast
And all the birds seemed to sing
While I listened to that one heavy bird
Thudding at the centre of our happiness.

But everything is torn away,
The clothes which were young and gay
Lie like dolls in attics
When the children have grown and ceased to play;
Or they fall with Autumn leaves
When fashions are blown out on white sales
Before the models of another day.

That great bed on which there lies
The charming haunting animal
Is a torrent that carries away
All the nests and singing branches
Tangled among blocks of ice
Which were the springs of yesterday.

Unless our love has wiser ways
Than the swallow glancing on
The azure summer surface,
To go when the waves rise.
– O hold me in that solemn kiss
Where our lips are changed to eyes
And in the deep lens of their gaze
Smiles and tears grow side by side
From the loving stillness.

Variations on My Life

To knock and enter
Knock and enter
The cloudless posthumous door
Where the slack guts are drawn into taut music
And there to sit and speak
With those who went before;

And to be justified
At last being at their side
To know I have no quality
Of ultimate inferiority
But bear on rounded shoulders the weight of my
    humanity;

To look down on my life
And see a life
Sociable puppet painted with a mouth
And to give the mouth a voice
That is not death
But its own truth confessing its own justice;

And to accept
My own weakness beyond dispute
Which is the strength I reject
Reaching back to the past with a dark root
Where earth and womb connect.

*

There is never enough air
There is never a wide enough space
There is never a white enough light
There is never a three-dimensional paper
Where the praise may loop like an aeroplane:

To knock and enter
Knock and enter
The room white as paper
With light falling on a white space
Through high windows of power
On hands resting on the controlling table,
Hands severed from the wrists
Moving only with the thoughts in fingers;

And to find release
From the continual headache
And the necessity of such long journeys;
The necessity of being alone
And the never being alone
Away from the lighted cities of the brain;

To touch and kiss
The gold horizon of the withheld wish;
To enter the flower of those who fructify
And fall and fade in the night full of desire;
To know the physical enduring secret
Strength whispers to the acrobat;

And to enter
The cold frigate voyaging to despair:
For this also is life, this also
Is the journey to the wonderful snow.
What hunger! And what distances!
Here is far more than coldness
That so illumines the whole surface!
Here is the crystal microscopic rose
That out of the frozen nerve grows.

Oh, but to ride on
The whole quivering human machine!
Less efficient than an aeroplane
Rather, a feathered, artificial bird
Which hardly flies but holds our lives

In all its love.
Oh to be taken by it, and to hold
My ear against its ever-female heart,
And to accept its fleas and all its sins,
To explore all its gifts
And nothing, nothing to refuse.

To say I love and I forgive
And that I know all that I hold;
Never to slide
Away among the drawing-rooms and hatred
From what it gives –
That is to walk in a sacred grove

And pluck the ripened voices with their ears
Bound into sheaves filled with the sun
Of summers that spoke and then went on;
And among them to place
My own posthumous voice
Which nothing does refuse
And only death denies.

Variations on My Life

THE SECOND

. . . or to return
To the first loved friend, you
Whose life seemed most unlike my own
As though you existed on an island
In seas of an archaic time,
Hidden under birdsong and olive trees,
With eyes chiselled to reflect the sky,
And behind the blue the clear flame,
And the hoarded quietness
Of summer at evening that surrounds a wood

Loaded with thunder,
Whose gentleness withholds the trigger
Night and tiger.

If I could return
And with a gained balance of happiness,
The scales of a golden success,
Smile and reassure you and undo the unhappiness
I wound around us then;
If I had a common Midas touch,
The fingers of an electric sign –
As I remember you stood once
In the tar-streaked drizzling street
With the light on your hair,
Smile painted by a day
Neither yours nor mine.

And if I could cease to demand,
As I asked then,
I know not what demonstrable favour
Nor what invented want,
For I have this to offer –
I was the sea, I was the island
Where the casqued heroic head
Lay and was remembered;
My innocent crystal mirrored your heart,
My mind was your legendary sky of love.

If I could accept
Myself in those in whose
Sweetness my life dissolves
And trust they could accept
Themselves in me; nor fear
Their expert quick disfavour
At the way I frown or hold my head;
Nor the smiling easy rivals
In whose faces the South winds blow,

And who become most serious
When the night and dance revolve.

O, then my body would enter
Its island and its summer
The questions find their answer
And my head its resting-place
Where the other heart lies
Washed by the seas of blood
Under the trees and clouds
And the healing sky
Of the breast's breathing space.

And I would know the peace
Of some distant frequent face
Seen in street or train,
Full of withheld promise,
Which out of rapid day
Enters the tunnel of my dream
Endowed with every wish
And then is dragged away
Into rapid day again.

Napoleon in 1814

Your heart was loaded with its fate like lead
Pressing against the net of flesh: and those
Countries that crept back across the boundaries
Where you had forced open the arena
Of limelit France with your star at the centre,
Closed in on you, terrified no longer
At the diamond in your head
Which cut their lands and killed their men.

You were the last to see what they all saw
That you, the blinding one, were now the blind
The Man of Destiny, ill destined.

For, as your face grew older, there hung a lag
Like a double chin in your mind. The jaw
Had in its always forward thrust
Grown heavy. The bones now drove
Towards a bed. But to sleep there, the peace
Must sign with blood the sheets of Russian snow.

Your quicksilver declaiming eye
Had frozen to the stare of a straight line
Which only saw goals painted in its beam
And made an artificial darkness all around
Which thickened into Allies.

Before, you were the genius whom all envied
An image of the self-delighting child
On his mother rosily seizing all
Till he was buried in stiff clothes and ruled
By a dead will becoming his own will. In you
The Caesars tamed by dying, fired again
Their lives in the unlegendary sky
With all the vulgar violence of Today.
And secretly you were much loved by all
Whose eyes sailed deep into their mirrors
To see whether a mouth culled like a flower
Might burst into Napoleon.

Then suddenly you ceased to be the prayer
Of hidden self to self. You changed into that one
Whom all the world looks at from the outside:
The nurse's bogey and the dragon
With scaly flanks gaped at by villagers
Smashing the harvest with its lashing tail.
Even the brutes could not imagine
The monstrousness of being you.

Men spoke of you as Nature, and they made
A science of your moods.
Your way of always marching forward

To fight a battle, and still marching on,
Was known like winter and like winter
Answered with a numbness all around
On which the boughs of a charred Moscow hung
Offering no life or food.

Your fate became your Elba where you stood
Upon your armies like a voyaging rock.
The world broke round, deep in its anger, yet
Transparent to your sun, salt, barren, tugged
By hidden tides of power and gold,
And with a flattering tongue that finally drowned.

Your generals fell out of your head like hair,
The tinsel victories from your gleaming laurels,
And your face became a glass
Where all looked through on to your losses.
The statesmen you had overthrown
Sprouted again in their gold leaves
And watched you shrivel back into a man.
O your heart beat the drum out that was you

Yet it felt something put aside, perhaps
Your youth, perhaps your throne – that piece of wood.
O your body still was brass
Around a trumpet mouth. O, it could call
The Guards out of their graves; four hours,
Which lost you Paris, back from yesterday;
Or multiply the cannon balls,
Those genitals of death;
O if you stretched your arm, you'd stretch out France.

All your thoughts were pouring yesterdays
With blood and flags and smoke and men
To fill the hollows of today.
Being all memory, you forgot
The narrow shaves of time. But the lean world,
Famished by you, and eating back again

Upon your fall, in all its bones and hunger
Was – like the unemployed that stare
With eyes from the stone edges – avidly Tomorrow.

The kings of yesterday might still have saved
Your throne for you – because you were a king.
If one, touching your shoulder,
Could persuade you to measure
Your claims against your present power,
The stature of your body in a mirror,
And not against that superhuman shadow
Struck by the sunset across your empire.

Yes, if he took you to the glass
And said 'Look'. But you would not see a map,
Nor would you see yourself. You'd see
Yourself and fate; and those commands
That once were armies, as the lines on your face,
And ghostly as the history in men's brains.
The world had been your language which you wrote
In carnage and the rape of lands.
The lines on the white paper followed after,
In thin black letters, what your lines
Of men wrote on the world.
But now the armies had crumbled and the words

Had caught up all the deeds and left behind
You with the wreck of deeds, the empty words,
As though you'd learnt yourself by heart
And knew nothing but that great rhetoric
Once echoing the thunder of the field
But now hidden in the hollow bones.

Yet what you made the world was always you
In your own mind, and what you won
In lands, you wrote upon men's brains:
And now that all was lost, it sprang again
Where in your heart already, Waterloo
Purely persisted, like an echo.

The Mask

Involved in my own entrails and a crust
Turning a pitted surface towards a space,
I am a world that watches through a sky
And is persuaded by mirrors
To regard its being as an external shell,
One of a universe of stars and faces.

My life confronts my life with eyes, the world
The world with lenses: and the self-image
Lifted in light against the lens
Stares back with my dumb wall of eyes:
The seen and seeing softly mutually strike
Their glass barrier that arrests the sight.

But the world's being hides in the volcanoes
And the foul history pressed into its core;
And to myself my being is my childhood
And passion and entrails and the roots of senses;
I'm pressed into the inside of a mask
At the back of love, the back of air, the back of light.

The other lives revolve around my sight
Scratching a distant eyelid like the stars;
My life, my world, scarcely believes they live;
They are the mirrors of the foreign masks
Stamped into shapes, obedient to their laws
Following a course till death completes their arc.

Houses at Edge of Railway Lines

To rise up and step out
Of the lurid shrieking cinder
Travelling more miles than minutes to the hour,
Iron on iron through the iron night
And its iron full of fire;

To rise up and throw away its will
Straight as a Roman frown
Joining a town to another town,
Falling through the night in an age of bombs
And full of tender watching eyes

Fixed on floodlit thoughts in magazines
Or sinking to their stomachs full of plans
Or searching for hope on the horizon,
The beam of a lost dawn,
Or browsing on furnace fires of doom;

And without knocking to enter
The life that lies behind
The edges of drawn blinds,
A sun behind the clouds
Of slums, suburbs and farms
Where love fills rooms, as gold
Pours into a valid mould.

A woman takes down her hair
Electric in the room
And fills her linen night-gown
As the air fills a balloon;
And her lover does not ask
For the window of the stage
Which opens on the eyes
Of the star-gazing critics,
For their love rests in the furrows
Of her wrinkled brow,
Lying there, as a line
Is laid on earth by the plough.

And heat and untidy hair
And beads of sweat on the skin
And the accepted smells,
His eyes buried in her breasts
Like rough quartz in a mine,

Make a forgiveness
Within the turning night
Of trains and frosts outside,
So tall and rushing else.

To a Spanish Poet

(for Manuel Altolaguirre)

You stared out of the window on the emptiness
Of a world exploding:
Stones and rubble thrown upwards in a fountain
Blasted sideways by the wind.
Every sensation except loneliness
Was drained out of your mind
By the lack of any motionless object the eye could find.
You were a child again
Who sees for the first time things happen.

Then, stupidly, the sulphur stucco pigeon
Fixed to the gable above your ceiling
Swooped in a curve before the window
Uttering, as it seemed, a coo.
When you smiled,
Everything in the room was shattered;
Only you remained whole
In frozen wonder, as though you stared
At your image in the broken mirror
Where it had always been silverly carried.

Thus I see you
With astonishment whitening in your gaze
Which still retains in the black central irises
Laughing images
Of a man lost in the hills near Malaga
Having got out of his carriage
And spent a week following a partridge;

Or of that broken-hearted general
Who failed to breed a green-eyed bull.

Beyond the violet violence of the news,
The meaningless photographs of the stricken faces,
The weeping from entrails, the vomiting from eyes,
In all the peninsular places,
My imagination reads
The penny fear that you are dead.

Perhaps it is we who are unreal and dead,
We of a world that revolves, dissolves and explodes
While we lay the steadfast corpse under the ground
Just beneath the earth's lid,
And the flowering eyes grow upwards through the grave
As through a rectangular window
Seeing the stars become clear and more clear
In a sky like a sheet of glass,
Beyond these comedies of falling stone.

Your heart looks through the breaking body,
Like axle through the turning wheel,
With eyes of blood.
Unbroken heart,
You stare through my revolving bones
On the transparent rim of the dissolving world
Where all my side is opened
With ribs drawn back like springs to let you enter
And replace my heart that is more living and more cold.

Oh let the violent time
Cut eyes into my limbs
As the sky is pierced with stars that look upon
The map of pain,
For only when the terrible river
Of grief and indignation
Has poured through all my brain
Can I make from lamentation

A world of happiness,
And another constellation,
With your voice that still rejoices
In the centre of its night,
As, buried in this night,
The stars burn with their brilliant light.

1939

Archaic Head

If, without losing this
Confidence of success,
I could go back to those days
And smile through that unhappiness
I wound about us then –
You would see what I now give
Whose intolerable demand
Then, was to touch your hand.
You would see what I have given:
This particular island
Where your archaic head
Is found, having been buried:
Hacked out with words, and read.

Auf dem Wasser zu Singen

A girl today, dreaming
On her river of time
With April clouds streaming
Through the glass of her eyes,
Laid down her book,
Looked shoreward, and sighed:

'Oh, if print put on flesh
And these words were whispers
From the lips of the poet
In the vase of my face,
Then this punt would be the river
That bore my name for ever
And my legend never fade.

'Then I would understand
What the people of his land
Never understood: his heart

Was torn apart
By a vulture: hence
Fury his address,
And his life disorder.

'I would cling tight to his hand –
The handle of the glass
Where my image would pass
And I saw my face for ever,'
She thought, turning from her lover
Whose need then hung above her.

And he looked up
Across a gulf of rivers
Straight into a face
High above this time and place
And the terrible eyes knew him
And his terrible eyes knew them.

'After the wrestling, when our mouths'

After the wrestling, when our mouths
Had kissed to heal their wounds,
And both sides victory gained, then peace was signed
And on my burning body you drew
With grateful hands the shining folds
Of a cloth stretching from head to heel,
Invisible lineaments I wear,
Pressing my face against my arm
To touch and smell your body there.

[1939]

Letter from the G.O.M.

Sir! I raise my pen and I raise my head
I look without flinching at the sun.
We did not say what you think we said
We did not do what you hoped we'd done.

I met a whore in Trafalgar Square
And she looked at me with a bold stare
And just as I would with the whole population
I talked, ignoring her rank and station.

'Hypocrite!' you accuse. That's what, day by day,
My opponents from their back benches say
But when I raise my sombre eye
Their little tattered pennons fly.

Hypocrite you! at the end of my time
Like a sweeper's ghost on the streets of our city
With a gritty eye and a nose of slime
Blasting them with your respectability.

Yes – if you'd know – for a generation
Bound by a private and public fetter
To a loving wife and a hating nation
I've served both – faithful – to the letter.

Yes – if you'd know – when I saw that girl
There was a sap in a root I felt stir
And I watched a spiritual sail unfurl
At the shaking of her ostrich feather.

The time I sprang from had roots indeed;
The great men with the country names
Were the trees which bore the seed –
Not gelded for fear of public shames.

The girl I spoke with used a word
A Pitt, unblushing, might have heard;

Her lips were soil for the language
Of a feasting, writing age.

When I looked at her body a moon flowered;
She could put the years off with her dress –
This century rolling away like a cloud
To reveal that original loveliness.

RUINS AND VISIONS (1942)

Song

Stranger, you who hide my love
    In the curved cheek of a smile
And sleep with her upon a tongue
    Of soft lies which beguile,
        Your paradisal ecstasy
    Is justified is justified
By hunger of all beasts beneath
    The overhanging cloud,
        Who, to snatch quick pleasures run,
        Before their momentary sun
Be eclipsed by death.

Lightly, lightly from my sleep
    She stole, our vows of dew to break,
Upon a day of melting rain
    Another love to take;
        Her happy happy perfidy
    Was justified was justified
Since compulsive needs of sense
    Clamour to be satisfied
        And she was never one to miss
        The plausible happiness
Of a new experience.

I, who stand beneath a bitter
    Blasted tree, with the green life
Of summer joy cut from my side
    By that self-justifying knife,
        In my exiled misery
    Were justified were justified
If upon two lives I preyed

Or punished with my suicide,
        Or murdered pity in my heart
        Or two other lives did part
To make the world pay what I paid.

Oh, but supposing that I climb
        Alone to a high room of clouds
Up a ladder of the time
And lie upon a bed alone
        And tear a feather from a wing
And listen to the world below
And write round my high paper walls
        Anything and everything
Which I know and do not know!

A Separation

Yes. The will decided. But how can the heart decide,
Lying deep under the surface
Of the level reasons the eye sees –
How can the heart decide
To banish this loved face for ever?

The starry eyes on the fringe of darkness
To forgo? The light within the body's blindness?
To prove that these were lost in any case,
And accept the stumbling stumps of consolations,

When under sleep, under the day,
Under the world, under the bones,
The unturning changeless heart,
Burning in suns and snows of passion,
Makes its mad protestations
And breaks, with vows and declarations?

The Vase of Tears

Tears pouring from this face of stone,
Angels from the heart, unhappiness
From some dream to yourself unknown –
Let me dry your eyes with these kisses.
I pour what comfort of ordinariness
I can; faint light upon your night alone.
And then we smother with caresses
Both our starved needs to atone.

Stone face creased with human tears: yet
Something in me gentle and delicate
Sees through those eyes an ocean of green water
And one by one the bitter drops collects
Into my heart, a glass vase which reflects
The world's grief weeping in its daughter.

The Double Shame

You must live through the time when everything hurts
When the space of the ripe, loaded afternoon
Expands to a landscape of white heat frozen
And trees are weighed down with hearts of stone
And green stares back where you stare alone,
And the walking eyes throw flinty comments
And the words which carry most knives are the blind
Phrases searching to be kind.

Solid and usual objects are ghosts
The furniture carries cargoes of memory,
The staircase has corners which remember
As fire blows red in gusty embers,
And each empty dress cuts out an image
In fur and evening and summer and gold
Of her who was different in each.

Pull down the blind and lie on the bed
And clasp the hour in the glass of one room
Against your mouth like a crystal doom.
Take up the book and look at the letters
Hieroglyphs on sand and as meaningless –
Here birds crossed once and cries were uttered
In a mist where sight and sound are blurred.

For the story of those who made mistakes
Of one whose happiness pierced like a star
Eludes and evades between sentences
And the letters break into eyes which read
What the blood is now writing in your head,
As though the characters sought for some clue
To their being so perfectly living and dead
In your story, worse than theirs, but true.

Set in the mind of their poet, they compare
Their tragic bliss with your trivial despair
And they have fingers which accuse
You of the double way of shame.
At first you did not love enough
And afterwards you loved too much
And you lacked the confidence to choose
And you have only yourself to blame.

The Journey

Upon what confident iron rails
    We seemed to move to the clear view
At the end of the line, where, without fail,
    My visions would come true.

There, where the sun melts the curved hills
    In one transparent wave against the skies,
I'd see your tender smile, more than your will,
    Shine through the coldness of your eyes.

Our harsh tongues of today would run in tears
    Back to this buried Now become the past.
In the cool shadows we'd unclasp our fears
    Transformed to love at last.

Oh, but then suddenly the line
    Swung onto another view
Barren with myself, and the blank pain
    Of the crammed world without you.

A Hall of Mirrors

Into a hall of mirrors
A hall of many mirrors
I enter,

Searching for that one face
Of innocence: amongst your many faces
Endlessly repeated in the empty spaces
Of your own eyes;
Suspended thinly on threads
Of your own self-admiring gaze.

At last, at last, when the light drops
From the glass tongues of praise,
In the dark your eyes are afraid,
Cowering at the bottom of a sad and lonely pit,
And your head like a doll's on your arm falls.

Yet a voice flowers from your sleep
And Venus throbs through your shut eyelids.
I search through a tunnel of past years
For a child who stands quite alone
Fallen from the care of the world's hands,
Exposed to all her fears,
Her face bright as a fruit with wet tears,
And I fall down shafts of love

Into the abyss of something human
Something lost when the long nights advance,
Hidden behind the hands of chance.

I search deep in the wells of weakness
And I read the innocence beyond the lie
The truth behind the evasive eye,
The terrible lost innocence
Fluttering faintly in a distant dance,
And the truth that stands, and begs forgiveness.

Till I drown, drawn down by my own mercy.

Somewhere in the night, above the branches
Restless with tongues of leaves over the square,
Where you and I and all
The false play-acting puppets are,
In a high room, hidden in the darkness,
There lies your heart, the truly good,
Swathed in the flesh where all roses unfold,
Warm in the nest which is the root of beds,
Surrounding me with love like all the stars
Blessing a birth with seed of fires,
O, waiting with an infinite gift
Which to refuse to search and find
Is to be cold and cruel and blind.

No Orpheus, No Eurydice

Nipples of bullets, precipices,
Ropes, knives, all
Now would seem as gentle
As the far away kisses
Of her these days remove
– To the dervish of his mind
Lost to her love.

There where his thoughts alone
Dance round his walls,
They paint his pale darling
In a piteous attitude standing
Amongst blowing winds of space,
Dead, and waiting in sweet grace
For him to follow, when she calls.

For how can he believe
Her loss less than his?
'True it is that she did leave
Me for another's kiss;
Yet our lives did so entwine
That the blank space of my heart
Torn from hers apart,
Tore hers too from mine.'

O, but if he started
Upon that long journey
Of the newly departed
Where one and all are born poor
Into death naked,
Like a slum Bank Holiday
Of bathers on a desolate shore;

If, with nerves strung to a harp,
He searched among the spirits there,
Looking and singing for his wife
To follow him back into life
Out of this dull leaden place,
He would never find there
Her cold, starry, wondering face.

For he is no Orpheus,
She no Eurydice.
She has truly packed and gone
To live with someone
Else, in pleasures of the sun,

Far from his kingdoms of despair
Here, there, or anywhere.

A Wild Race

I

I know a wild race
Foreign to their own time
Estranged from their loved
And hating home place.

Inhabitants of dead languages,
They still live in intact quarters
Of cities and speeches.

From ashen parchment
And corroded stone
Their bearded thoughts
Are still outspoken,

Out of dust and bone
The broken unbroken.

For their teeth stamped words
Which still flash with eyes
Where, whiter than paper,
Their day dazzles libraries.

And they were as far
From their contemporaries
As the living today
From those are.

Far as the stars
Whose out-of-the-past light
Ravishes tonight's night
With their present-piercing future.

II

Their unloved love
Luminous with words
Like a sun burned
Through the transparent body
Of their day's beauty
For which they yearned.

Their endless need
And their timeless gift
Lay on the light eyelids
Of their self-seeking
Feminine city
Like a reproach, weighed
With immortality.

The beloved, afraid,
Laughed, and betrayed.

III

But a girl today, dreaming
On her wave of time
With April clouds dawdling
Through the mirror of her eyes,
Lays down her book
And smiles and sighs
Lifting her empty head
Across the gulf of centuries:

'O, if print put on flesh
And these words were whispers
From the lips of the poet
In the vase of my face,
Then this wave would be a river
Where my name would float forever
And my flower never fade.

'O, I would understand
What his own time and land
Never knew: that his heart
Was torn apart
By loss large as a vulture: hence
The black fury of his dress
And his hair in disorder.

'O, I would take his hand
And his words would be my mirror
Where I saw my face forever.'
She thinks, turning from her lover
Whose need then hung above her
Like an eagle in the air.

And across the gulf of time
The cold terrible snow mountains
Saw his naked heart alone
And they knew him
And he knew them.

The War God

Why cannot the one good
Benevolent feasible
Final dove descend?

And the wheat be divided?
And the soldiers sent home?
And the barriers torn down?
And the enemies forgiven?
And there be no retribution?

Because the conqueror
Is an instrument of power,
With merciless heart hammered
Out of former fear,
When today's vanquished
Destroyed his noble father,
Filling his cradle with anguish.

His irremediable victory
Chokes back sobbing anxiety
Lest children of the slain
(When the ripe ears grow high
To the sickles of his own
And the sun goes down)
Rise in iron morning
To stain with blood the sky
And avenge their fathers again.

His heart broke before
His raging splendour.
The virgins of prayer
Fumble vainly for that day

Buried under ruins,
Of his pride's greatest murder
When his heart which was a child
Asking and tender,
He hunted and killed.

The lost filled with lead
On the helpless field
May dream the pious reason
Of mercy, but also
Their eyes know what they did
In their own proud season,
Their dead teeth bite the earth
With semen of new hatred.

For the world is the world
And not the slain
Nor the slayer, forgive,
Nor do wild shores
Of passionate histories
Close on endless love;
Though hidden under seas
Of chafing despair,
Love's need does not cease.

To Poets and Airmen

(Dedicated to Michael Jones in his life, and now in his memory)

Thinkers and airmen – all such
    Friends and pilots upon the edge
Of the skies of the future – much
    You require a bullet's eye of courage
    To fly through this age.

The paper brows are winged and helmeted,
    The blind ankles bound to a white road

Streaming through a night of lead
   Where cities explode.
   Fates unload

Hatred burning, in small parcels,
   Outrage against social lies,
Hearts breaking against past refusals
   Of men to show small mercies
   To men. Now death replies
Releasing new, familiar devils.

And yet, before you throw away your childhood,
   With the lambs pasturing in flaxen hair,
   To plunge into this iron war,
Remember for a flash the wild good
   Drunkenness where
   You abandoned future care,

And then forget. Become what
   Things require. The expletive word.
   The all-night-long screeching metal bird.
And all of time shut down in one shot
   Of night, by a gun uttered.

The Air Raid across the Bay

I

Above the dead flat sea
And watching rocks of black coast
Across the bay, the high
Searchlights probe the centre of the sky
Their ends fusing in cones of light
For a brilliant instant held up
Then shattered like a cup.

They rub white rules through leaden dark,
Projecting tall phantom

Masts with swaying derricks
Above the sea's broad level decks.

They slide triangles and parallels
Of experimental theorems,
Proving the hypothesis
Of death, on wasted surfaces
Of measureless blank distances.

II

But through their gliding light-streams,
    An invisible ragged sound
Moves, trailed by two distraught beams.
    A thudding falls from remote cones
And pink sequins wink from a shot-silk screen.

    Seeds of killing drop on cells of sleep
Which hug these promontories like dark-brown winkles.

Fingers pick away
Human minds from hollow skulls.

III

The shining ladders slant
Up to the god of war
Exalted on those golden stilts
And riding in his car
Of a destroying star.

But the waves clucking in the rocks
And the sacred standing corn
Brittle, and swaying with metallic clicks,
Their secret wealth lock
In an elemental magic
Of ripeness, which mocks
The nails through flesh torn.

Winter and Summer

Within my head, aches the perpetual winter
Of this violent time, where pleasures freeze.
My inner eye anticipates forever
Looking through naked trees and running wheels
Onto a blank transparent sky
Leading to nothing; as though, through iron aims,
It was stared back at by the filmy surface
Of a lid covering its own despair.
Thus, when the summer breaks upon my face
With the outward shock of a green wave
Crested with leaves and creamy foam of flowers,
I think the luxurious lazy meadows
Are a deceiving canvas covering
With a balmy paint of leafy billows,
The furious volleys of charioteering power
Behind the sun, racing to destroy.
    When under light lawns, heavy in their soil,
I hear the groaning of the wasted lives
Of those who revolve unreflecting wheels,
    Alas, I prove that I am right,
For if my shadowed mind affirmed the light
It would return to those green, foolish years
When to live seemed to stand knee-deep in flowers:
There, winter was an indoor accident,
Where, with head pressed against the glass, I watched
The garden, falsified by snow,
Waiting to melt, and become real again.

In Memoriam

The senseless drone of the dull machines in the sky
    In a chain extending the boundaries
        Of a distant invisible will,

Weaves a net of sound in the darkness on high
Drawing the senses up in one Eye
From our tunnelled entombed bodies,
Where everything stops but the wishes that kill.

Living now becomes withered like flowers
In the boring burned city which has no use
For us but as lives and deaths to fill
With fury the guns blazing back on the powers
That scorch our small plot of blasted hours:
Death we cannot refuse
Where everything stops but the wishes that kill.

Driven by intolerance and volted with lies,
We melt down the whirring bodies of boys
And their laughter distil
To plough metal hatred through the skies
And write with their burning eyes over cities
Sure no green summer joys,
Where everything stops but the wishes that kill.

Filled with swear words, laughter and fire,
Soothed by the girl hands and clothed in my words,
What, my fine feather-head, laughing lad Bill,
Was your life, but a curveting arc of desire
Ricochetting in flames on your own funeral pyre
Instinctive as birds,
Where everything stops but the wishes that kill?

June 1940

The early summer prepares its green feasts
In the garden, hot on the blossom of the peach,
Pressed close by bird song, crossed by bees,
Electrified with lizards; and the voices each to each

Speak, afloat on deck chairs. They say
How little they know of the battle far away
Different from the war in France in their day.

Beyond the hot red walls, the blowing
Of dust on dog roses in the hedges,
The meadows weighed with shadows, bringing
Youths with girls and bicycles, at evening
Round the War Memorials of villages;

Beyond the crisp sea, with lines
Engraved by winds and keels on glass dunes,
Perpetually moving and appearing still,
Tiring the eye with a permanent dance;
Far away! Divided by gleaming scissors
Of the steel channel – the raw edge of France.

Through their voices there moves a murmur like a ball
Rolled across the plains and hills,
Divided to ruffled whispers by the seas.

For the German caterpillar-wheeled dreams,
Imagined into steel, volley
Through the spring songs and the green hedges,
Crushing the lark's nest, with a roar of smoke,
Through the weak barriers of France.

'False is this feast which the summer, all one garden,
Spreads before the senses. Our minds must harden.'

'Nor ears nor eyes, but the will
Is the perceiving organ of the soul.
Man's world is not nature, but Hell
Where he struggles to make a nightmare whole.'

'History is a dragon under the soil
Wearing today only as a skin
Which man sloughs off when his dreams begin.'

'The season of our soul is doom
Born today from a terrible womb.'

'Yes, we see the dragon's teeth of the past
From a hungry childhood grown
Into avenging warriors at last.'

'Indolent injustice for so long
Snoring over Germany, now is overthrown:
To face *us* with a still greater wrong.'

'While we forgot, and the sun seemed to forgive,
Those bitter children were alive.
Their hatred never forgot to thrive.'

'Well, well, the greater wrong must meet
Tomorrow with a worse defeat.'

Afloat on the lawn, the ghastly last-war voices
With blue eyes gaze for a moment on this:
England chained to the abyss.

Then, altogether, they begin
To murmur: 'Of course, we shall win.'

But the voice of one who was young and died
In a great battle, in the light leaves sighed:

'I lay down with a greater doubt:
That it was all wrong from the start:
Victory and defeat both the same,
Hollow masks worn by shame
Over the questions of the heart.
And there was many another name
Dividing the sun's light like a prism
With the rainbow colours of an "ism".
I lay down dead like a world alone
In a sky without faith or aim
And nothing to believe in,
 Yet an endless empty need to atone.'

The Ambitious Son

Old man, with hair made of newspaper cutting
And the megaphone voice,
Dahlia in the public mind, strutting
Like a canary before a clapping noise,

My childhood went for rides on your wishes
As a beggar's eye strides a tinsel horse,
And how I reeled before your windy lashes
Fit to drive a paper boat off its course!

Deep in my heart I learned this lesson
As well have never been born at all
As live through life and fail to impress on
Time, our family name, inch-tall.

Father, how we both pitied those who had let
The emptiness of their unknown name
Gleam on a rose and fade on a secret,
Far from our trumpeting posthumous fame!

For how shall we prove that we really exist
Unless we hear, over and over,
Our ego through the world persist
With all the guns of the self-lover?

Oh, when the weight of Time's whole darkness
Presses upon our shuttered fall,
How shall we prove, if our lives went markless,
That we have lived at all?

But, my admired one, imagine my sorrow
When I watched the schoolboys' inquisitive faces
Turn away from your Day, and Tomorrow
Mock your forehead with sneering grimaces.

Soon you lay in your grave like a crumpled clown
Eaten by worms, by quicklime forgotten,
Fake, untragic, pelted down
By a generation still more rotten.

When I left the funeral, my face was hard
With my contempt for your failure still
But, Father, my hardness was a scabbard
Sheathing your undefeated will.

Behold, a star fled from your breast
Of death, into my life of night
Making your long rest my unrest,
My head burn with frustrated light.

Through my breast there broke the fire
Of a prophetic son's anointment
Seeking a fame greater than Empire.
It was then I made my appointment

With Truth, beyond the doors of Death.
How like an engine do I press
Towards that terminus of my last breath,
When all the Future you and I possess

Will open out onto those endless spaces
Where, from an incorruptible mine,
Yours and my name take their places
Among the deathless names that shine!

O Father, to a grave of fame I faithfully follow!
And yet I love the glance of failure tilted up
With swimming eyes and waiting lips, to swallow
The sunset from the sky as from a cup.

Often I stand, as though outside a wall,
Outside a beggar's face, where a child seems hidden,
And I remember being lost, when I was small,
In a vast, deserted garden.

If I had the key I might return
To where the lovers lie forgotten on bright grass.
The prisoners and the homeless make me burn
With homesickness when I pass.

Yes! I could drown in lives of weakness,
For I pity and I understand
The wishes and fulfilments under the dream surface
Of an oblivious and uncharted land.

The Drowned

They still vibrate with the sound
Of electric bells,
The sailors who drown
While their mouths and ships fill
With wells of silence
And horizons of distance.

Kate and Mary were the city
Where they lingered on shore
To mingle with the beauty
Of the girls: they're still there –
Where no numbness nor dumbness
Appals dance hall and bar.

No letters reach wrecks;
Corpses have no telephone;
Cold tides cut the nerves
The desires are frozen
While the blurred sky
Rubs bitter medals on the eyes.

Jack sees her with another
And he knows how she smiles
At the light facile rival
Who so easily beguiles

Dancing and doing
What *he* never will now.

Cut off unfairly
By the doom of doom
Which makes heroes and serious
Skulls of men all,
Where under waves we roll
Whose one dream was to play
And forget death all day.

The Fates

I

In the theatre,
The actors act the ritual of their parts,
Clowns, killers, lovers, captains,
At the end falling on the sword
Which opens out a window through their hearts
And through the darkness to the gleaming eyes
Of the watching masks slightly bored,

Of the audience
Acting the part of their indifference,
Pretending the thrusting pistons of the passions,
Contorted masks of tears and mockery,
Do not penetrate the surface fashions
Covering their own naked skins.

'We are not green fools nor black-eyed tragedians,
Though perhaps, long ago, we were the killers.
Still, still we have our moments of romance
Under the moon, when we are the lovers.
But the rules of fate do not apply to us.
The howling consequences can be bribed away
Discreetly, without fuss.

When we have left the play
The furies of atonement will not follow after
Our feet, into the street
Where the traffic is controlled all day.'

Sitting in stalls or pit, they pray
That the externalized disaster
Gesticulating puppets display
Will not, with finger of catastrophe
Revolve on them its hissing frontal limelight:
Not lift the curtains of their windows,
Not rape their daughters in the coarse embrace
Of the promiscuous newspapers
Running with them in headlines through the streets.
In their lives, they have cut few capers
So death, they hope, will be discreet,
Raising a silk hat,
Dressed in black, with a smile for each tear, polite.

Oh which are the actors, which the audience?
Those who sit back with a tear, a smile, a sigh,
Where they deny deny deny?
Or those on the stage who rip open their ribs
Lift the lids from their skulls, tear the skin from their arms,
Revealing the secret corridors of dreams,
The salt savour of the passions,
The crushed hyacinths of corruption,
The opera-singing sexual organs:
And within all, as in a high room,
Filled with a vacuum containing infinite space,
The soul playing at being a gull by a lake,
Turning somersaults, immensely bored,
Whistling to itself, writing memoirs of God,
Forgetting
What time and the undertakers undertake?

Oh which are the actors, which the audience?
The actors, who simulate?

Or those who are, who watch the actors
Prove to them there is no fate?
Where then is the real performance
Which finally sweeps actors and audience
Into a black box at the end of the play?

Both, both, vowing the real is the unreal,
Are stared at by the silent stars
Of the comprehensive universe
Staging its play of passions in their hearts.
It carries them off at the end in a hearse.

II

O brave, powdered mask of weeded motherhood
For twenty years denying that the real
Was ever anything but the exceptional,
You were an excellent stage manager,
For your dear son's sake, of your theatre,
Family life, not sombre, but light:
'This is the play where nothing happens that can matter
Except that we are sensible healthy and bright.'

Your problem was no easy one,
Somehow to spare your only son
From the gloomy brooding blue of his father's eyes,
After the War, for twenty years
Pacing the lawn between two wars,
His sombre way of staring at the table.
You were courageous and capable
Gaily you called these things his 'moods'.
Just 'moods', 'moods', like anything else,
A chair, the empty clanging of alarm bells.

You rebuilt the Georgian house with the old lawn,
And the kitchen garden surrounded by a wall,
And the servants in the servants' hall

Tidying the rooms downstairs at dawn;
And you bought a fishing rod, a pony and a gun
And gave these serious playthings to your son.

The fresh air and the scenery did the rest.
He ripened and his laughter floated on the lake,
A foretaste of the memories that now suggest
His photograph with the shirt open at the neck.
He came downstairs to dinner, 'dressed'.
Then your triumphant happiness bound cords
Around his silken glance into one bow.
Catching your husband's eye, your face spoke words
'This is the world, we've left the past below.'

If a guest came, and in the course
Of conversation, spoke of 'so-and-so's divorce',
Or else, 'Poor Lady X, she died of cancer',
You had your fine frank answer,
Questioning him with vivid curiosity,
Poverty, adultery, disease, what strange monstrosity!
You smiled, perhaps, at your guest's eccentricity
Dragging such specimens out on your floor.

Your son grew up, and thought it all quite real.
Hunting, the family, the businessman's ideal.
The poor and the unhappy had his sympathy.
They were exceptions made to prove his rule.
And yet he had his moments of uneasiness
When in the dazzling garden of his family
With the green sunlight tilted on your dress,
His body suddenly seemed an indecency,
A changeling smuggled to the wrong address.

Still, he got married. *She* was dull, of course.
But everything had turned out quite all right.
The bride sailed on the picture page in white
Arm linked in his, face squinting in the light.
Your son wore uniform. You, the mother-in-law

Who'd brought him up into a world at war,
At last felt tired. You wondered what he knew of life,
Whether enough to satisfy his wife.
Perhaps he'd learned from nature, or his horse.

III

Oh, but in vain
Do men bar themselves behind their doors
Within the well-appointed house
Painting, in designed acts, life as they would see it,
By the fireside, in the garden, round the table.

The storm rises,
The thunderbolt falls, and how feeble
Is the long tradition strengthened with reverence
Made sacred to respect by all appearance,
Or the most up-to-date steel-and-concrete
To withstand fate.

The walls fall, tearing down
The fragile life of the interior.
The cherishing fire in its grate
Consumes the house, grown to a monster,
As though the cat had turned into a tiger
Leaping out of a world become a jungle
To destroy its master.

The parents fall
Clutching with weak hands beams snapped like straw,
And the handsome only son,
Tanned leader of his village team,
Is shaken out of the soft folds
Of silk, spoiled life, as from a curtain.

He is thrown out onto a field abroad.
A whip of lead
Strikes a stain of blood from his pure forehead.

Into the dust he falls,
The virginal face carved from a mother's kisses
As though from sensitive ivory,
Staring up at the sun, the eyes at last made open.

At Night

During day's foursquare light
All is measured by eyes from the outside,
Windows look and classify the clothes
Walking upon their scaffolding of world.

But at night
Structures are melted in a soft pond
Of darkness, up to the stars.

Man's mind swims, full of lamps,
Among foundations of the epoch.
Clothes fade to the same curtains
As night draws over the blaze of flesh.

His heart – surrounded by money,
Loaded with a house, and hub-like
Centring spokes of fashionable change –
Grows dizzy at uncertainty,
At life longer than single lives,
At an opening out of spaces
Revealing stars more numerous
Than the overcrowded populace.

Every social attribute gained
Falls into the Milky Way.
The questions so long hidden
Behind the answers of the present
Rise from the superstitious past
Like ghosts from ruined palaces.

Into his hand of a single moment
There pour forgotten races
With eyes opening on plains like flowers,

And the unknown nations to come after,
Unthinkable as his own death dismissed
To the vanishing point of the future;

All are crushed into the bones of Now
Knit in his flesh of loneliness.

Oh, but his 'I' might glide
Here into another such 'I'
Invisible in nakedness;
His heart in the heart of darkness find,
Stretching from lonely birth to lonely
Death, like a mind behind the mind,
The image of his own loneliness,
The answering inconsolable cry
Of lost humanity,
Which the explicit day
Colours and covers and explains away.

The Barn

Half-hidden by trees, the sheer roof of the barn
Is warped to a river of tiles
By currents of the sky's weather
Through long damp years.

Under the leaves, a great butterfly's wing
Seems its brilliant red, streaked with dark lines
Of lichen and rust, an underwing
Of winter leaves.

A sapling, with a jet of flaming
Foliage, cancels with its branches
The guttered lower base of the roof, reflecting
The tiles in a cup of green.

Under the crashing vault of sky,
At the side of the road flashing past

With a rumour of smoke and steel,
Hushed by whispers of leaves, and bird song,
The barn from its dark throat
Gurgitates with a gentle booming murmur.

This ghost of a noise suggests a gust
Caught in its rafters aloft long ago,
The turn of a winch, the wood of a wheel.

Tangled in the sound, as in a girl's hair
Is the enthusiastic scent
Of vivid yellow straw, lit by a sun-beam
Laden with motes, on the boards of a floor.

In a Garden

Had I pen ink and paper,
I think that they could carry
The weight of all these roses,
These rocks and massive trees.

The hills weigh peacefully on my mind,
The grottoed skull encloses
Shifting lights and shade.
Soft on the flesh all the green scene reposes

But that the singing of those birds
Pressed to the hot wall of the sky,
Tears through the listening writing of the eye
To a space beyond words.

A Childhood

I am glad I met you on the edge
Of your barbarous childhood.

In what purity of pleasure
You danced alone like a peasant
For the stamping joy's own sake!

How, set in their sandy sockets,
Your clear truthful transparent eyes
Shone out of the black frozen landscape
Of those grey-clothed schoolboys!

How your shy hand offered
The total generosity
Of original unforewarned fearful trust,
In a world grown old in iron hatred!

I am glad to set down
The first and ultimate you,
Your inescapable soul. Although
It fade like a fading smile
Or light falling from faces
Which some grimmer preoccupation replaces.

This happens everywhere at every time:
Joy lacks the cause of joy,
Love the answering love,
And truth the objectless persistent loneliness,
As they grow older,
To become later what they were
In childhood earlier –
In a grown-up world of cheating compromises.

Childhood, its own flower,
Flushes from the grasses with no reason
Except the sky of that season.
But the grown desires need objects
And taste of these corrupts the tongue
And the natural need is scattered
Amongst satisfactions which satisfy
A debased need.

Yet all prayers are on the side of
Giving strength to innocence,
So I pray for nothing new,
I pray only, after such knowledge,
That you may have the strength to become you.

And I shall remember
You, who, being younger,
Will probably forget.

Into Life

Aiming from clocks and space,
      O Man of Flesh, I hew
         Your features, blow on blow.
I cut away each surface
      To lay bare what I know –
Universe within you.

Shut close in your mind,
   You never quite will learn
      To see your life as whole.
Your mirrors are too blind;
   They have no eyes that turn
      From each age on your soul.

Your sense flies to each facet
   Striking from each hour;
      Now all heat, now all brain,
   All sex, sickness, power;
That severe line, when I place it,
      Seems nothing but pain.

Yet all experience, like stars
   (In distances of night,
      Their brilliant separate incidents
Divided by light-years)

Hangs in your eyes the lights
   Of sustained co-existence.

What you were, you are,
   And what you will be, you are, too.
      Born, you're dead; loving, are sad.
The years add, star by star,
   The whole of life consuming you
      In fires of good and bad.

The Coast

These riding and ridden faces
Upon the wheels and tracks of trade,
With ruts where money runs; their talk
A metal traffic; bodies jolting trucks; their glances
Squinting six months ahead to count the profit,
Not a day beyond;
These in the streets, the dives, the shops, the City,

Inhabit this coast of rocks,
Poriferous stone expectorated on
By jellied spittle; rockpools lisping –
Blog, blah, fligger, fluck, fick, mallock.

Where the tide furls back shallow finny waves,
My swearing mates in their blue dungarees
Stand on the endless mud-flats reaching back
To their unscrupulous births. The sea
Will swill away the tag-ends of their names
With cards, and all that harbours do forget.

Would not, to open any door
Onto the star socketed in a skull,
Or through the domed night to the balanced scales,
Or following threads leading to faith
Sustained between two pairs of eyes:

Be false and frail as flowers
Crushed by iron machines of power?

Yet there are eyes which float upon the wreckage
Secretly clinging to a gleaming straw.
Some acts of kindness wave their handkerchiefs.
A trickling life runs through clogged veins
And streams flow backward buried under flesh.

A wind blows hither

Rest, rest, you ghoulish masks of life,
At last the fingers of the sky
Will lift the hard expressions from your tongues,
Unlock the mild sighs from your skulls,
Laugh with the laughter clinging to the marrow,
And knit you, flesh and bone,
Into a life of joy again.

Dusk

Steel edge of plough
Thrusts through the stiff
Ruffled fields of turfy
Cloud in the sky.
Above charcoal hedges
And dead leaf of land
It cuts out a deep
Gleaming furrow
Of clear glass looking
Through our funnelled day
Up a stair of stars.

On earth below
The knotted hands
Lay down their tasks,
And the wooden handles

Of steel implements
Gently touch the ground.
The shifting animals
Wrinkle their muzzles
At the sweet passing peace,
Like bells, of the breeze;
And the will of Man
Floats loose, released.

The dropping day
Encloses the universe
In a wider mantel
Than meridian blaze.
A terracotta blanket
Of dark, robs one by one
Recognition from villages,
Features from flowers,
News from men,
Stones from the sun.

All the names fade away.
With a spasm, nakedness
Assumes menkind.
Their minds, cast adrift
On beds in upper rooms,
Awaiting the anchorage
Of sleep, see more
Than a landscape of words.

The great lost river
Crepitates
Through creeks of their brains.
Long-buried days
Rise in their dreams.
Their tight fists unclose
The powers they hold,
The manners and gold.

Then the burning eye
Of a timeless Being
Stares through their limbs
Drawing up through their bones
Mists of the past
Filled with chattering apes,
Bronze and stone gifts,
From all continents
Of the tree of Man.

The sun of this night
Mocks their dark day
Filled with brief aims
– Stealing from their kind
And killing their kind.
Abandoning hope,
They turn with a groan
From that terror of love
Back to their daybreak of
Habitual hatred.

Daybreak

At dawn she lay with her profile at that angle
Which, sleeping, seems the stone face of an angel;
Her hair a harp the hand of a breeze follows
To play, against the white cloud of the pillows.
Then in a flush of rose she woke, and her eyes were open
Swimming with blue through the rose flesh of dawn.
From her dew of lips, the drop of one word
Fell, from a dawn of fountains, when she murmured
'Darling', – upon my heart the song of the first bird.
'My dream glides in my dream,' she said, 'come true.
I waken from you to my dream of you.'
O, then my waking dream dared to assume

The audacity of her sleep. Our dreams
Flowed into each other's arms, like streams.

To Natasha

You, whom such fragments do surround
    Of childhood straying through your face
Leaving two signs of hair there as your name –
        Through the loneliness
        Of my long look past the darkness
At the tunnel's end, I watch your curving neck,
The wondering colours marvel in your eyes,
My space of silence touch your dawn that lights
        My life's emerging line.

You, who are afraid of fear,
    Whose past has moulded hollows in your cheeks,
Who murmur 'mercy', turning in your sleep,
    Whose glances touch me with shy voices:
        Your fingers of music
        Pressing down a rebellion of mistakes
Raise here our devout tower of mutual prayer.

    I am one who knows each day his past
Tear out the links from an achieving chain;
    Daily through vigorous imagining
I summon my being again
        Out of a chaos of nothing.
My grasp on nothing builds my everything
Lest what I am should relapse into pieces.

Darling, this kiss of great serenity
Has cast no sheet anchor of security
    But balances upon the faith that lies
        In the timeless loving of your eyes
    Our terrible peace, where all that was

Certain and stated, falls apart
　　Into original meanings, and the words
That weighed like boulders on us from the past
Are displaced by an earthquake of the heart.

1942–1944

Elegy

Within each one, is the unfolding will
Of the universal and the human.
The sun unfolds the hidden light within.
The distant ploughing stars till
The isolation of a birth
Upon the enclosed field of man and woman.

Each, in his body, recreates the earth
Which, with memory, is transparent.
Through books, towers, jugs (behind the vast
Encroaching wall of the past)
The dead are apparent.

'In my limbs, Life, be fruitful.
Cultivate me with your South.
Sun assist, and sapient Love
Through my buds and branching move.
Let the words add on my mouth
The inner to the outer whole.
Grant me time, place, peace, affection
To ripen into your perfection.'

Thus each prays. But the tiger rages
Pitting his will against their wills.
His iron claws tear out the pages
From the innocent story, rhyme from rhyme.
Singly, in each, the whole he kills.
He tears the days and minutes out of time.
Credulous buds he ravages.

'The tiger is yourself,' accuses
The naked dawn of steel skies.
And the heart of each one, lost to innocence,
Knows murder in the glass of his own eyes.
It roars up through the root of nightmares

And through the grace of love it stares
When a gesture falters and a word confuses.

Alone, each traces the reason
To the existence of his neighbours.
Those abroad gun here their jealousy.
The dead are convicted of treason.
This one is rich. That poor one labours.
Hatred of each by each is policy.

Till hatred, like the moon, queen of the night,
Torn from the roots of life, climbs to the centre
Of the hollow skull, and weaves the dream
Which is the hard unspoken motive
Behind the surface eye that seems.
Her light against the light enters
Human passion, to seek and find a votive.

Each one attends her gleaming steel machines
Giving himself, and taking what she gives,
Shut in his body's time and place and means.
The superficial moments when he lives
Smiling in love or truth, are but the masks
Worn over hollow emptiness inside,
While he pursues the blind malignant tasks
Which all pursue, and each from each divide.

He toils in factories of destruction.
His play is – to forget. Monster despairs
Cover the earth, scrabbling like the seas'
Waste unassuageable friction.
His greatest torture is his thirst for peace,
The sterile changeless thirst within, that wears
More than the lines of change upon his face.

But when that nozzled polished death he made
For each, by each is aimed at last at him,
Suddenly through slits of eyes and ears

He is transfixed by all the universe,
Withered by stars when day is dim
Into a great space of humility,
While through the convex hood of gathering shade
Vanish the lost lights of the human city.

[1942]

Prague Dressed in Light

From the Czech of Jaroslav Seifert,
by Stephen Spender and Jiří Mucha

I walked in the late dusk one day
– Then Prague seemed lovelier than Rome –
This dream would never pass away
I thought, and I not wake, when come
Stars from their daylight place of hiding
The winged, armed gargoyle, whose dark form is
Under the old cathedral cornice
Like a sentinel protruding.

One day I walked in the first dawn
(I thought it useless to sleep more)
The bolt of the great gate was drawn
I was afraid to knock the door.
Alas, the pilgrim waits outside
The spring morning with no key!
The gargoyle I had wished to see
At dawn, when the stars cease to hide.

But I saw a grave; and I went to it:
Being alone, I had no fears.
Like a wreck was the dead man's shoe: its
Tip was pointing towards the stars.
Above the sleeping brow, when the flame

Trembled, I saw the shadow steal.
And I could hear the spinning wheel
And, from the vineyard, singing came.

We wove in the mantle of the king
Grapes gray as human breath at dawn.
In the nave, four ladies sleeping
The dead one on their breasts have borne.
Greet the woods round Castle Tyn
Falling gently into the plain
O greet that Karluv Tyn again
And the hillsides flowing with wine.

From his deep grave, he raised above
The pillars grown under his palm,
A white skull: made only for love
His hands which loved it were a balm.
It was made sacred by the song
Of the people, with parched lips;
It strengthened him, a charm that slips
From the great heirloom wrecked so long.

How could his lips do else than parch?
Ceaselessly on a sword he slept.
For ages past the chorale march
With ardent watch his surety kept.
The saint is covered with the wings
Of angels, and a shield of prayer.
He broke white bread which the poor share
And crushed grapes with his feet, a king's.

Dazed near the Majesty so great,
Towards the beggars' doors I creep.
I did not come to weep into the agate,
The time has passed when I could weep.
A broken stand opens the music.
Someone has torn the embroidered altar.

The heels of boots, without falter,
Hollow on the gold mosaics, click.

[1943]

The Statue of Apollo

One night I slept with the statue of Apollo.
I adored first the concave furrows of his thighs
In whose hard hollows my ripe fists lay.
His breast and his cheek-bones, chiselled
By lines of trilling flutes, I stroked.
Then he melted from stone to marble
And from marble to burning alabaster,
His lips pressed my lips, and he exclaimed:
'I love you because you create song in words
And I am rounded from music.' I held his hand
And between his ribs and through his chest spread
The fusing powerful rays of a moon
Which I saw, beyond the stars of his nipples
And the patina of his skin suspended like a shield.
I cried: 'I understand you. O do not forget me.'
Then he arose, with the trumpets of the sunrise,
And departed for ever, as heroes do always.

[1943]

Bridle of the Sun

Sun is a millstone in the sky.
We are enmeshed in inextricable day,
Packed in this multiple July
By a million grinding seeds of fire
In stubble, kilns, hedgerow, sky.

197

Even in this day, whose aims,
Abstract and metallic, chase
Through every second – this day
All one time and one place –
Even in this day, we inhabit
Our own small physical climate:
And we cannot see over the edges
Of flesh, clocks and hedges,
Being lashed by the sun to one date.

[1943]

Perfection

No one is perfection, yet
When, being without you, I console
Myself, by dwelling on some blemish
In you, once marked, which seems to mar the whole,
Telling myself your absence might become my wish,

Oh, then, that icy thought I set
Between ourselves, thaws, shrivels, vanishes,
When I remember how your eyes
Lighten often on mine, wonderful skies,
Melting with forgiveness and gentle wishes.

Arrowy light suffuses mist,
And lapis lazuli has kissed,
With burning eyes, a way through cloud,
Detailing the green valley homes below which seem
The world illuminated by the dream,
Love's dazzling head transcendant in a shroud.

[1944]

Paris

From the French of Louis Aragon

Where there is good in the storm's heart of rage
Where in the heart of the night it is fair
The air is alcohol and misfortune courage
Windowframes broken hope still glimmers there
And from ruined walls the songs climb the air.

Never extinguished reborn from its blaze
Eternal glow of our motherland this
From Point du Jour until Père Lachaise
In August most sweet reflorescent of rose trees
Folk of everywhere the blood of Paris.

There's no *éclat* like Paris this dust under
Nothing so pure as her brow's resurgent wave
Nothing is so strong not fire nor thunder
As my Paris her dangers defiant to outbrave
Nothing so lovely as this Paris I have.

Nothing before made my heart to beat thus
Nothing my laughter with my tears so mated
As this cry of my people victorious
Nothing is so vast as a shroud torn and shed
Paris, Paris, of herself liberated.

[1944]

POEMS OF DEDICATION (1947)

These poems are inscribed to the memory of Margaret Spender
who died on Christmas Day, 1945

I

Darling of our hearts, drowning
In the thick night of ultimate sea
Which (indeed) surrounds us all, but where we
Are crammed islands of flesh, wide
With a few harvesting years, in our own lives disowning
The bitter salt severing tide;

Here in this room you are outside this room,
Here in this body your eyes drift away,
While the invisible vultures feed on
Your flesh, and those who read the doom
Of the ill-boding omens say
The name of a disease which, like a villain

Seizes on the pastures of your life
Then gives you back some pounds of flesh, only again
To twist you on that rack of pain
Where the skeleton cuts through you like a knife,
And the weak eyes flinch with their own weak light
Of hope, which blinds our hoping watching sight.

Until hope signs us to despair – what lives
Seems what most kills – what fights your fate
Loses most strength – and the loved face which smiles
Mirrors the mocking illness which contrives
Moving away some miles
To ricochet again at the fixed date.

Least of our world, yet you are most our world
Here where the well are those who hide
In dreams of life painted by dying desire
From violence of our time outside;

Where those who most live are most often hurled
With heroic eyes through waters shot with fire.

Where sailors' eyes rolling on floors of seas
Hold in their fading darkening irises
The vision of some lost still living girl
The possible attainable happy peace
Of Europe, with its pastures fertile,
Dying, like a girl, of a doomed, hidden disease.

So, to be honest, I must wear your death
Next to my heart, where others wear their love.
Indeed, it is my love, my link with life
My word of life being death upon my breath.
My dying word because of you can live
Crowned with your death, so not evading truth.

II

(*To H.S.*)

Dearest and nearest brother,
No word can turn to day
The freezing night of silence
Where all your dawns delay
Watching flesh of your Margaret
Wither in sickness away.

Yet those we lose, we learn
With singleness to love:
Regret stronger than passion holds
Her the times remove:
All those past doubts of life, her death
One happiness does prove.

Better in death to know
The happiness we lose
Than die in life in meaningless

Misery of those
Who lie beside chosen
Companions they never choose.

Orpheus, maker of music,
Clasped his pale bride
Upon that terrible river
Of the ghosts who have died.
Then of his poems, the uttermost
Laurel sprang from his side.

When your red eyes follow
Her body dazed and hurt
Under the torrid mirage
Of delirious desert,
Her breasts break with white lilies,
Her eyes with Margaret.

As child, of those who played
With me, I sought you most:
Our twining hands and leafy eyes
Under world-schemes are lost;
And the kiss that reconciled
No longer spares the cost.

I bring no consolation
Of the weeping shower
Whose final dropping jewel deletes
All grief in the sun's power:
You must watch these things grow worse
Day after day, hour after hour.

Yet to accept the worst
Is finally to revive
When we are equal with the force
Of that with which we strive
And having almost lost, at last
Know that such was to live.

As she will live who, candle-lit,
Floats upon her final breath,
The ceiling of the frosty night
And her high room beneath,
Wearing not like destruction, but
Like a white dress, her death.

III

From a tree choked by ivy, rotted
By kidney-shaped fungus on the bark,
From out a topmost branch
A spray of leaves is seen
Spreading against the metal sky its mark,
As though the dying tree could launch
The drained life of the sap
Into the shoot of one last glance
Above the lapping shining discs of evergreen.

So with you, Margaret,
Where you are lying,
The strong tree of your limbs dragged back
By harsh cords of regret,
And the golden sorrowful flesh
Scorched by hot disease,
How difficult is dying
In your living, dying eyes!

How tediously the clock kills
When your fading breath
Launches one usual word
Above the rigid body of death.
A trickling water fills
The sad well of your body
With gradual drops of dying

– Yet all the love we knew
Still smiles on your eyes.

Oh how, when you have died,
Shall I remember to forget
And with knives to separate
Your death from my life –
Since, darling, there is never a night
But the restored prime of your youth
With all its flags does not float
Upon my sleep like a boat,
With the glance which will live
Inescapably as truth.

IV

Poor girl, inhabitant of a strange land
Where death stares through your gaze,
As though a distant moon
Shone through midsummer days
With the skull-like glitter of night:

Poor child, you wear your summer dress
And your shoes striped with gold
As the earth wears a variegated cover
Of grass and flowers
Covering caverns of destruction over
Where hollow deaths are told.

I look into your sunk eyes,
Shafts of wells to both our hearts,
Which cannot take part in the lies
Of acting these gay parts.
Under our lips, our minds
Become one with the weeping
Of the mortality
Which through sleep is unsleeping.

Of what use is my weeping?
It does not carry a surgeon's knife
To cut the wrongly multiplying cells
At the root of your life.
It can only prove
That extremes of love
Stretch beyond the flesh to hideous bone
Howling in hyena dark alone.

Oh, but my grief is thought, a dream,
Tomorrow's gale will sweep away.
It does not wake every day
To the facts which are and do not only seem:
The granite facts around your bed,
Poverty-stricken hopeless ugliness
Of the fact that you will soon be dead.

V

    (i)

Already you are beginning to become
Fallen tree-trunk with sun-burnished limbs
In an infinite landscape among tribal bones
Encircled by encroaching ritualistic stones.

    (ii)

Those that begin to cease to be your eyes
Are flowers parched of their honey where memories
Crowd over and fly out like avid butterflies.
The striped and glittering colours of lost days,
Swallow-tail, Red Admiral, fritillaries,
Feed on your eyes and then fly from our gaze.

(iii)

In the corner of the bed you are already partly ghost
A whispering scratching existence almost lost
To our blatant life which spreads through all the rooms
Our contrast transient as heaped consoling blooms.

(iv)

You are so quiet; your hand on the sheet seems a mouse.
Yet when we look away, the flails
Which pound and beat you down with ceaseless pulse
Shake like a steam hammer through the house.

(v)

Evening brings the opening of the windows.
Now your last sunset throws
Shadows from the roots of all the trees,
Atrean hounds it unleashes
In front of a sky in which there burns a rose.
The Furies point and strain forwards.
The pack of night is crowding towards us.

VI

The final act of love
Is not of dear and dear
Blue-bird-shell eye pink-sea-shell ear
Dove twining voice with dove:

Oh no, it is the world-storm fruit,
Sperm of tangling distress,
Mouth roaring in the wilderness,
Fingernail tearing at dry root.

The deprived fanatic lover,
Naked in the desert

Of all except his heart,
In his abandon must cover

With wild lips and torn hands,
With blanket made from his own hair,
With comfort made from his despair,
The sexless body in the sands.

He follows that bare path
Where the flesh guides to the skull
And the skull into hollows, full
Of delirium and death.

Dazed, he sees himself among
Saints, who slept with leprous sins,
Whose tongues grow on such ruins
And such a wild fire is his tongue –

'How far we travelled, sweetheart,
Since that day when first we chose
Each other as each other's rose,
And put all other worlds apart.

'Now we assume this coarseness
Of loved and loving bone
Where all are all and all alone
And to love means to bless
Everything and everyone.'

(*To Natasha*)

Summer

The midsummer glow
Reflected in her eyes
Is colour of clover
In grass flesh where she lies.
Bird-shadow cloud-shadow
Draw a net of sighs
Over her from her sun-gold lover.

Through the August days
She drinks his acres of light
Which, quivering through dark dreams
Beyond mind-sight and eye-sight,
Reach a womb where his rays
Penetrate her night,
In brilliant black commingling streams.

What pallor ah what dearth
When August's flesh,
Kaleidoscope of flowers
And September's rusted fetish
Are lidded under earth!
Then the eyes vanish
With fair forgotten withered harvest hours.

Four Eyes

The core of the day
Is these twin spheres of eyes
Where cloud, stone, clover,

All things beheld, stay,
World of summer which lies
Buried in loved and lover.

He reads in her gaze
Words inscribed by her sight
On stone and clover, those dreams
Which sprang from his praise.
Through their four eyes, light
Of world and world streams.

Alas, what dearth
Of sun, when clasped flesh,
With coronals of flowers,
Charioteer under earth –
O eyes which were a mesh
To net the summer hours!

The Dream

'You dream', he said, 'because of the child
Asleep in the nest of your body, whose dreams
Flutter through your blood in streams.'

Her lips dreamt, and he smiled.

He laid his head, weighed with a thought
On the sleep of her lips. Thus, locked
Within the lens of their embrace
They watched the life their lives had wrought
The folded future active street
With walls of flesh and crowning face,
Within her flesh complete,
Between their clinging bodies rocked.

Man and Woman

Through man's love and woman's love
Moons and tides move
Which fuse those islands, lying face to face.
Mixing in naked passion
Those who naked new life fashion
Are themselves reborn in naked grace.

The Trance

Sometimes, apart in sleep, by chance,
You fall out of my arms, alone,
Into the chaos of your separate trance.
My eyes gaze through your forehead, through the
   bone,
And see where in your mind distress has torn
Its violent path, which on your lips is shown
And on your hands and in your dream forlorn.

Restless, you turn to me, and press
Those timid words against my ear
Which thunder at my heart like stones.
'Mercy', you plead. Then 'Who can bless?'
You ask. 'I am pursued by Time', you moan.
I watch that precipice of fear
You tread, naked in naked distress.

To that deep care we are committed
Beneath the wildness of our flesh
And shuddering horror of our dream,
Where unmasked agony is permitted.
Our bodies, stripped of clothes that seem,
And our souls, stripped of beauty's mesh,
Meet our true selves, their charms outwitted.

This pure trance is the oracle
That speaks no language but the heart.
Our angel with our devil meets
In the atrocious night, nor do they part
But each each forgives and greets,
And their mutual terrors heal
Within our love's deep miracle.

Absence

No one is perfection, yet
When, being without you, I console
Myself, by dwelling on some blemish
Once marked, which now might mar the whole,
Telling myself your absence might become my wish,

Oh then, that blemish which I set
Between us, vanishes.
I see only the pure you in your eyes,
Remembering how they light
With mine. All that between us lies
Is opened like a gate
Through which our memories unite
The oneness of their wishes.

Absence has the quality of ice
On a high peak, above a landscape of snow:
It is a freezing lens which magnifies
The valley of the roofs and hearths below.
Each twig and footprint shows in glassy outline
Of black and white which simplifies
Like passion. Blank light shines
On the home faces, surrounding them with white
As though flesh were the halo of the eyes.

Arrows of light pierce through the mist,
Lapis lazuli has pressed

Its burning way through smothering cloud
To show upon the world your face which seems
A miracle among macabre dreams,
Like a madonna painted on a shroud.

Lost

Horizontal on amber air three boughs of green
Lift slotted sleeves. Beyond them, the house glows.
Straight mouldings delineate tall windows.
Glass panes weigh the balance between
Garden mirrored and interior darkly seen.

That cracked stucco wall seems the rind
Of miles and days from here to what I savour:
My thought, biting it, penetrates the flavour
Of a shining withheld day behind
Where sweetness entered me, body and mind.

Against that wall my eating memories press
As though through my own flesh into my heart.
One room, my heart, holds a girl with lips apart
Watching a child starred in his nakedness.
Her gaze covers him like a fleecy dress.

That is the room where the world was most precious
Where jewelled silence on their eyes collects
The light which each from each reflects.
Here lamp and wooden furniture are gracious.
All other times and places seem atrocious.

My spirit shut outside them is a ghost
Gazing through clay and gales at his warm past.
From out my empty everywhere I cast
My seeing unseen eyes through the time lost
Back to that one room where life was life most.

PART THREE: SPIRITUAL EXPLORATIONS

(*To Cecil Day Lewis*)

    We fly through a night of stars
Whose remote frozen tongues speak
A language of mirrors, diamond Greek
Glittering across space, each to each –
O dream of Venus and Mars,
In a dome of extinct life, far far far from our wars.

I

Within our nakedness nakedness still
Hollows our minds. Past and stars show
Through the paper skulls. Tomorrows blow
Away the fabrications of the will.
    The Universe, by inches, minutes, fills
Our tongues and senses, name and image glow
With word and form. Star and history know
That they exist in our lives existence kills.
    Revolving with the earth's rim through the night
We fragments pulsing blood and breath,
Each separate in consciousness, reunite
In that dark journey to no place or date,
Where, naked beneath nakedness, beneath
Our divided condition, all await
The multitudinous loneliness of death.

II

You were born; must die; were loved; must love;
Born naked; were clothed; still naked walk
Under your clothes. Under your skin you move
Naked: naked under acts and talk.
    The miles and hours upon you feed.
They eat your eyes out with their distance
They eat your heart out with devouring need
They eat your death out with lost lost significance.
    There is one fate beneath those ignorances,
Those flesh and bone parcels in which you're split,
O thing of skin and words hanging on breath:
Harlequin skeleton, it
Strums on your gut such songs and merry dances
Of love, of loneliness, of life being death.

III

Since we are what we are, what shall we be
But what we are? We are, we have
Six feet and seventy years, to see
The light, and then resign it for the grave.
    We are not worlds, no, nor infinity,
We have no claims on stone, except to prove
In the invention of the human city
Our selves, our breath, our death, our love.
    The tower we build soars like an arrow
From the world's rim toward the sky's,
Upwards and downwards in a dazzling pond
Climbing and diving from our world, to narrow
The gap between the world shut in the eyes
And the receding world of light beyond.

IV

We divided, join again in belief.
　We feel the indivisible knots which bind
Each separately: the ends which blind
The eye revolving inwardly in grief.
　Each circular life gnaws round its little leaf
Of here and now. Each is tied within its kind.
Also nature outside within the mind
Tempts with its tree each one to be a thief.
　Mortals are not aeons, they are not space,
Not empires, not maps: they have only
Bodies, and graves. Yet all the past, the race,
Knowledge and memory, are unfurled
Within each separate head, grown lonely
With time, growing, shedding, the world.

V

The immortal spirit is that single ghost
Of all time, incarnate in one time,
Which through our breathing skeletons must climb
To be within our supple skin engrossed.
Without that ghost within, our lives are lost
Fragments, haunting the earth's rim.
Unless we will it live, that ghost pines, dim,
Lost in our lives; its life, our death, the cost.
　One being of present, past, futurity,
Seeks within these many-headed wills
To release the flame-winged dove, humanity.
Shut in himself, each blind, beaked subject kills
His neighbour and himself, and shuts out pity
For that one winging spirit which fulfils.

VI

I am that witness through whom the whole
Knows it exists. Within the coils of blood,
Whispering under sleep, there moves the flood
Of stars, battles, dark and frozen pole.
All that I am I am not. The cold stone
Unfolds its angel for me. On my dreams ride
The racial legends. The stars outside
Glitter under my ribs. Being all, I am alone.
  I who say I call that eye I
Which is the mirror in which things see
Nothing except themselves. I die.
The things, the vision, still will be.
Upon this eye reflections of stars lie
And that which passes, passes away, is I.

VII

Outside, the eternal star-tall mountains gleam
Where changeless changing past and future lock
Their fusing streams into one day of rock
Against whose day my days but shadows seem.
  Within my shut skull flows a historied stream
Of myths, fears, crimes, that hammering stock
Which hews my limbs out of the daylight block
And makes my lives the slave of their past dream.
  The Universe, the dead, humanity, fill
Each world-wide generation with the sigh
Which breathes the music of their will.
Their sensitive, perceiving witness, I,
See mirrored in my consciousness, the ill
Chameleonic harlequin who'll die.

VIII

Light
Light
Burning through eyes and windows
Of the body the will the house

Knife
Knife
Thread-suspended over clasped locked flesh
Where the demoniac powers
Dreaming of power, enclose
The ruinous and to-be-ruined life

Bright
Bright
With lightening compact in dark hours
Strike down tear apart unlock expose
The feud the kiss the will the heart
Of this people imprisoned in night
Their gods mad
Their princes fanged with revenge poisonous and bad
Lost and lolling among the shadows.

Strike to the womb the unborn with new power
Speak to the boy back from the sword-bright war
And with his wounds unbandage his light eyes
Show him him as he is
Show him your own existence as you are
Teach him his blindness teach him to rise
Show him his body and what winged steed
Fulfilments of your grace and his grace need.

Show him the words that bleed
Out of the past and through the present
To the future of his heirs-apparent
Words and Pegasus he must guide
For generation of his generation to ride.

Tell him he does inhabit
Himself yourself, his spirit your spirit,
And let your purposes his purposes
Unfold through buds of him their flowers.

Through walls he builds and towers
O be your truth transparent
Make his hands burn with your burning roses.

Midsummer

(*To Edith Sitwell*)

There is midsummer
  Opens all the windows
And drowns the houses
  In fever of dust and rose.

Vibrant transparency above
  The hills, is visible.
All night the stars shake through the silence,
  Tangible, audible.

Clear day, you trail
  Whispers of cherry and rambler.
Sun, you'll gild the leaves to wraiths
  Withered in amber.

Within our distraught gale of time
  My secrecy listens
To a dynamo of summer that revolves
  Generating what glistens –

Noon, the moon, straws of light,
  Ringed pulsations on the lake,
Quietness folded on window sills,
  The loads the reapers make.

Would I might be that bough tonight
  Will dip in dews! And, wrung
From my impregnated phosphorescence,
  Honeyed song of my tongue!

But I am tied on strips of time,
  Caged in minutes, made

By men, exiled from the day's brilliance
    In a deliberate shade.

Only, some moment slips between the bars
    Of the raging machines.
It gleams with eternal rumours
    Of the high, midsummer scenes.

Man is that prison where his will
    Has shut without pity
In a clock eternity,
    In his fist, rose of infinity.

Seascape

(*In memoriam M.A.S.*)

There are some days the happy ocean lies
Like an unfingered harp, below the land.
Afternoon gilds all the silent wires
Into a burning music of the eyes.
On mirroring paths between those fine-strung fires
The shore, laden with roses, horses, spires,
Wanders in water, imaged above ribbed sand.

The azure vibrancy of the air tires
And a sigh, like a woman's, from inland
Brushes the golden wires with shadowing hand
Drawing across their chords some gull's sharp cries
Or bell, or gasp from distant hedged-in shires:
These, deep as anchors, the silent wave buries.

Then, from the shore, two zig-zag butterflies,
Like errant dog-roses cross the hot strand
And on the ocean face in spiralling gyres
Search for foam-honey in reflected skies.
They drown. Witnesses understand
Such wings torn in such ritual sacrifice,

Remembering ships, treasures and cities.
Legendary heroes, plumed with flame like pyres
On flesh-winged ships fluttered from their island
And them the sea engulfed. Their coins and eyes
Twisted by the timeless waves' desires,
Are, through the muscular water, scarcely scanned
While, above them, the harp assumes their sighs.

Meeting

Que mon amour a la semblance
Du beau Phénix, s'il meurt un soir
Le Matin voit sa Renaissance.
Apollinaire

I

At dawn we rose and walked the pavement

I your shadow you my flute

Your voice wove a thread
Through the city in my head

I followed – followed
You, my sole inhabitant.

II

'At last,' you sang, 'there comes this peace
Beyond war's separating will
Where we are alone, face to face.

'When tomorrow divides us, we shall fill
That space with this peace as now the space
Which, when we are closest, divides us still.

'Distances between us will be crystal
Traversed with illuminating rays
Where our eyes fuse the rainbow of their gaze.

'Gazing into that crystal, behold the possible
Nakedness nakeder than nakedness
Where, stripped of time and place as of a dress,
We meet again, being invisible,

'Farewell –'

    III

            Then the sun scrawled
Across the white sheet of the day
Twisted iron black realities
Broken boulevards through which humanity's
Sprawling river Styx
Of corroding shadows crawled.

O but our love was the Phoenix

Above the destroyed city reborn city
Conjoining spires of flame
Tower of wings climbing spear-shaken skies,
Within the ensphered luminous air of eyes
Image by our faith sustained the same.

    IV

Your mind and mine became one vase
Where gaze flowed into gaze
Under the surfaces
Of our curved embraces.

Our eyes see with each other's eyes
Though half a world between us lies.

Your night holds my light
My day is shuttered by your night.

These words enclose your silences.
One crystal gazes in our distances.

When we sleep, our separate dreams
Flow into each other's streams
Wave over far wave slips
Our lips melt into our lips.

On my tongue your tongue
Rustles with your song my song.

v

Into my heart there sprang these words
I no sooner uttered
Than they seemed in their concords
Not mine I said, but yours I heard.

These distances which separate
Drove our lives through that gate
Beyond which our impossible
Presences became invisible,
Our meeting indivisible.

THE EDGE OF BEING (1949)

To Natasha

O Omega, Invocation

O, thou O, opening O,
Passing from earth into a sky
Drained of last wings,
Then beyond the empyrean blue
Passing passing through light
Into space too white for seeing –

O, thou O, passing beyond
Light, into sound,
Where one trumpet sustains
Concentrated symphonies
On the peak of one note,
Then passing passing beyond
To all sound silence –

O, thou O, beyond silence
Invoking gods and goddesses,
The owl-eyed, the up-finger-pointing,
Imaged flesh changing
From idea into form
Then back to bodilessness,
Continual metamorphosis
Of gods changing to godlessness –

O, thou O, returning to
Thyself, O, whose black
Hoop, circling on white
Paper, vanishes where the eye
Springs through thee, O,
Beyond space silence image,
O thou, word of beginning
Oh with what wordless end.

O Night O Trembling Night

O night O trembling night O night of sighs
O night when my body was a rod O night
When my mouth was a vague animal cry
Pasturing on her flesh O night
When the close darkness was a nest
Made of her hair and filled with my eyes

(O stars impenetrable above
Each fragile life here where it lies
Among the petals falling fields of time
O night revolving all our dark away)

O day O gradual day O sheeted light
Covering her body as with dews
Until I brushed her sealing sleep away
To read once more in the uncurtained day
Her naked love, my great good news.

On the Third Day

(*To W.H.A.*)

On the first summer day I lay in the valley.
Above rocks the sky sealed my eyes with a leaf.
The grass licked my skin. The flowers bound my nostrils
With scented cotton threads. The soil invited
My hands and feet to press down and grow roots.
Bees and grasshoppers drummed over
Crepitations of thirst rising from dry stones,
And the ants rearranged my ceaseless thoughts
Into different patterns forever the same.
Then the blue wind fell out of the air
And the sun beat down till I became of wood
Glistening brown beginning to warp.

On the second summer day I climbed through the forest
(Huge tent anchored to the mountainside by roots)
My direction was defeated by weight of numbers
I could not see the wood for the trees.
The darkness lay under the leaves, in a war
Against light, which occasionally penetrated
Splintering spears through several interstices
And dropping bright clanging shields on the soil.
Silence was stitched through with thinnest pine needles
And bird songs were stifled behind a hot hedge.
My feet became as heavy as logs.
I drank up all the air of the forest.
My mind changed to amber enclosing dead flies.

On the third summer day I sprang from the forest
Into the wonder of a white snow-tide.
Alone with the sun's wild whispering wheel
Grinding sparks of secret light on frozen fields,
Every burden fell from me, I threw the forest from my back,
The valley dwindled to a human world departed,
Torn to shreds by clouds of the sun's shifting visions.
Above the snowfield, one rock against the sky
Shaped from utter silence a black naked tune,
A violin when the tune forgets the instrument
And the use of the ear is only as gate
To receive into the mind the sound's soundless form.

Awaking

Ever the same, forever new!
The gravel path searching the Way;
The cobwebs beaded with the dew;
The empty waiting of new day.

So I remember each new morning
From childhood, when pebbles amaze.

Outside my window, the forewarning
Glitter of those days.

The sense felt behind darkened walls,
An amber-solid world, a lake
Of light, through which light falls.
It is this to which I wake.

Then the sun shifts the trees around
And overtops the sky, and throws
House, horse and rider to the ground
With knockout shadows.

The whole sky opens to an O,
The cobweb dries, the petals spread,
The clocks grow beards, the people go
Walking over their graves, the dead.

The world's a circle where all moves
Before after after before.
Such joy my new-awaking proves
Each day – until I start to care.

[1930–1948]

Faust's Song

Oh, that I might be one with that moonlight
Which spreads its tiger stare across these books,
Through the high barred pane where, night after night,
My endless longing meets her endless looks!

Freed from these cobwebs, dust and phials of knowledge,
Would I might in her hell of heaven flit:
Be stripped in dews and rolled through grass and hedge
And sigh in caverns of her sensual spirit.

To wake on peaks at dawn among the inhuman
Rose-towering dreams – O peacocks, fountains, sighs –

Reborn in the blonde landscape of a woman,
And dying in the river of her eyes!

Judas Iscariot

The eyes of twenty centuries
Pursue me along corridors to where
I am painted at their ends on many walls.
     Ever-revolving futures recognize
This red hair and red beard, where I am seated
Within the dark cave of the feast of light.
     Out of my heart-shaped shadow I stretch my hand
Across the white table into the dish
But not to dip the bread. It is as though
The cloth on each side of one dove-bright face
Spread dazzling wings on which the apostles ride
Uplifting them into the vision
Where their eyes watch themselves enthroned.
     My russet hand across the dish
Plucks enviously against one feather
– But still the rushing wings spurn me below!

     Saint Sebastian of wickedness
I stand: all eyes legitimate arrows piercing through
The darkness of my wickedness. They recognize
My halo hammered from thirty silver pieces
And the hemp rope around my neck
Soft as that Spirit's hanging arms
When on my cheek he answered with the kiss
Which cuts forever –
                    My strange stigmata,
All love and hate, all fire and ice!

     But who betrayed whom? O you,
Whose light gaze forms the azure corridor
Through which those other pouring eyes

Arrow into me – answer! Who
Betrayed whom? Who had foreseen
All, from the first? Who read
In his mind's light from the first day
That the kingdom of heaven on earth must always
Reiterate the garden of Eden,
And each day's revolution be betrayed
Within man's heart, each day?

                        Who wrapped
The whispering serpent round the tree
And hung between the leaves the glittering purse
And trapped the fangs with God-appointed poison?
Who knew
I must betray the truth, and made the lie
Betray its truth in me?

     Those hypocrite eyes which aimed at you
Now aim at me. And yet, beyond their world
We are alone, eternal opposites,
Each turning on his pole of truth, your pole
Invisible light, and mine
Becoming what man is. We stare
Across two thousand years, and heaven, and hell,
Into each other's gaze.

Ice

(To. M.M.B.)

She came in from the snowing air
Where icicle-hung architecture
Strung white fleece round the baroque square.
I saw her face freeze in her fur
And my lips seemed to fetch quick fire
From the firelit corner of the room
Where I had waited in my chair.

I kissed this fire against her skin
And watched the warmth make her cheeks bloom
While at my care her smiling eyes
Shone with the health of the ice
Outside, whose brilliance they brought in.
That day, until this, I forgot.
How is it now I so remember,
Who, when she came indoors, saw not
The passion of her white December?

Returning to Vienna, 1947

(To W.J.S.)

I

Feminine Vienna, where the Ring's
Inner street embossed with palaces
Guarded the city virginal cathedral –

And in the central Graben Square
The swaggering column of a monument
Burst out of the past to commemorate
Some long-forgotten once-resisted rape
Whether by plague or Turk I now forget –

I saw the soot-stained marble battering-ram
Uplift its cloud of cherubim
Clustering on its cross like bees
Perpetually reborn virginities
Vienna ascendant against dissolving cloud –

Through summers of between-war dream
Vienna lay upon its plain
Each war one hand on the horizon's rim –

Summer already seemed hallucination
Of leaves painted upon a canvas screen

Behind which wicked forces laid
Their plot to end all summers –

Obscene kisses
Of first and second wars clucking
Behind the hedge of leaf-eyed lovers
Made boys' flesh conjuring their girls of rose
Their very lust sign of the time's decay
Their innocence sign of its impotence
By contrast with that breeding of steel furies –

Preparing a world's childless juvenescence.

II

Yet there the flower of my first flesh unfolded
Among her woods her cafés her stone draperies
There my youth was an eyed prow descrying
Beyond the storms of my crossed years
A fleshscape woven of fiery fleece –

Vienna of my loving my first woman
She and I had senses canopied
With luminous trilling leaves of beech
Knotted to boughs against transparent skies –

When I laid my head against her dress
Scented with flesh and porous with cicadas
Beyond the dark I saw the brooched lights shine
Within the earth I heard the deep warm pulse
Vienna's life was lying in my arms
While music shaping through me was the airs
Yearning through Vienna woods
To chisel sculpture of orchestras.

III

Beyond herself-myself   Beyond
Our interpenetrated human forest

Swallowing the absence in our meeting places
Beyond the vowing lipped abandonment
Of both to one meeting loneliness
Beyond the crystal bowl of our joined gaze –
There was reality, the flaw
Within the golden crystal bowl, where life
Was not entirely love nor even
Baroque frozen in dolphin attitudes
But was the unemployed who starved –

We saw their burning bodies like the spokes
Of cartwheels thrown down near dried ponds
We saw that prearranged disorder
Where socialist heroes who denied their souls
To hammer from their time-bound bodies
A world where workers would wear haloes
Each of his gain for what he gave –

Were shot at by the white-faced cynics
Who with their iron and stiff arms destroyed
These little optimists of tenements –

We saw the small empiric saints shot down
Shot down singing in their tenements
Their Karl Marx Hof and Goethe Haus
Killed by the realists of disenchantment.

IV

There where our love seemed hewn like crystal
Into a bowl where all times met
Within the stillness created by our looking –
Where the vision of the dead seemed absolute
Frozen within centennial architecture
Which futures rubbed like breezes over leaves
Lacing some lines and cherishing some gold –

The seeming permanence was an illusion
For what was real was transitory dust

True to our time dust blowing into dust
The dust a vital inward spring with power
To shatter history-frozen visions
And burst through cities and break down their walls –

The great stones of Vienna were but blocks
Lying across the present dissolution
Against that powerful decadence as weak
As senile oaths stuttering into dust –
And plunging deeper into our eyes' bowl
I saw there in our gaze what breaks the heart –

The tears and bloodshot vein of seeing
The outer world destroy the inner world.

v

Throughout that summer there was still some glory
Sunset lucidity which bathed
The Graben's cloud-insulting monument
And statues of extravagant angels
Wrestling in marble from the marble past
Perpetually reflowering virginal
Vienna against dissolving dust –

Gilded amid Baroque I mourned
The ruined shell of Karl Marx Hof and wept
The fallen workers amongst the ruined angels –

Their tears of pearl rolling down cheeks of gold
Changing to diamonds where they splashed the pavement –

And murdered Wallisch seemed a martyr
With raised right hand and marble frown
Moving in death through shell-torn tenements –

His hand with dying gesture signed
Such white and simple freedoms as could be
Chiselled on palaces for all humanity –

Where noble pasts with noble futures fuse.

VI

Vienna Vienna fallen in Vienna –

Within one instant of one night
One flash which made the streets one white –

Within one flash of time one knife
That held Vienna mirrored on its blade –

Then plunged – a hilt of diving wings –
To break the image into fragments –

The statued angel fell upon her knees
Agony shrouded with collapsing roofs

Her dereliction strewn before her history
Her marble feet broken –

      Then roared
The chariot of the smoking wide explosion
Dragging Vienna in tumbrils round her Ring –

Vienna Vienna fallen within Vienna.

VII

I come back to the fallen to the dust
The broken stones the wood splintered to straw
Which burst from the dismembered body –

The fragments torn out of the ruins
Are magic torn out of my mind
Are vision torn out of my eyes
Are spirit torn out of my soul –

And what the ruins leave which I can think
Into the city of my brain
Is forced abstractions and tired memories
A senseless lightless voiceless theatre
Where the ghosts play at being ghosts –

The old at wading waist-deep in the dust
The young at being lustreless –

My own existence dwelling in my body
Seems like an odour sicklied under rubble

A taste of marrow in the taste of bones
Tormented into apathy by shame –

The shame of what I never was
That when I lived my life among these dead
I did not live enough –

                      that when I loved
Among these dead – I did not love enough –
That when I looked the murderers in their eyes
I did not die enough –

                  I lacked
That which makes cities not to fall
The drop of agonizing sweat which changes
Into impenetrable crystal upon crosses
Which bear cathedrals –

                the will
Which breathes its upward music into domes
Through flutes of springing columns –

                the love
Which holds each moment to each moment
With architecture of continual passion.

Weep, Girl, Weep

Weep, girl, weep, for you have cause to weep.
His face is uprooted from your sleep,
His eyes torn from your eyes, dream from your dream.
Where you were by the window all one night

A million stars wore too faint a light
To show his machine
Plunge dark through dark out of sight.

    The wet tears on your face gleam
Down spires of the cathedral,
And in the crowded squares your lament
Makes a great angel whose instrument
Is strung on the heart behind the face of all.

The Angel

(To W.G.)

Each is involved in the tears and blood of all.
Under the dreams of each move those unsleeping journeys –
The Will, the Lament, the Fall.

We have no inviolate instants where we are
Solid happiness hewn from day, set apart
From the others afar.

Human islands under their seas have roots
Spread through the multitude's fretful blood,
And to passionate childhoods.

To steel the will against awareness would banish
The angel who arrives each instant
From the horrific flesh;

Who warns that power, fear, agony, are the life under many;
That the real is the terrible; that to deny
This, unsheathes tyranny.

Listen, for his voice offers charity, hope, freedom –
Beggared charity, false hope, freedom to weep. True, and yet
He is truth's own doom
Blowing news of evil on a golden trumpet.

Epilogue to a Human Drama

When pavements were blown up, exposing nerves,
And the gas mains burned blue and gold
And stucco houses were smashed to a cloud
Pungent with mice, dust, garlic, anxiety:
When the reverberant emptied façades
Of the palaces of commerce,
Isolated in a vacuum of silence, suddenly
Cracked and roared and fell, and the seven-maned
Golden lions licked the stony fragments:

Then the only voice through deserted streets
Was the Cassandra bell which rang and rang and ran
As if released at last by time
Towards those fires that burst through many walls –
Prophetic doom opened to the nostrils,
Blood and fire streaming from the stones.

The City burned with unsentimental dignity
Of resigned wisdom: those stores and churches
Which had glittered emptily in gold and silk,
Stood near the crowning dome of the cathedral
Like courtiers round the Royal Martyr.
August shadows of night
And bursting days of concentrated light
Dropped from the skies to paint a final scene –
Illuminated agony of frowning stone.
Who can wonder then that every word
In burning London seemed out of a play?

On the stage, there were heroes, maidens, fools,
Victims, a chorus. The heroes were brave,
The rescued appeared passively beautiful,
The fools spat jokes into the skull of death,
The victims waited with the humble patience
Of animals trapped behind a wall

For the pickaxes to break with sun and water.
The chorus assisted, bringing cups of tea,
Praising the heroes, discussing the habits of the wicked,
Underlining the moral, explaining doom and truth.

Rejoice in the Abyss

(*To F.C.C.*)

When the foundations quaked and the pillars shook
I trembled, and in the dark I feared
The photograph my skull might take
Through the eye sockets, in one flashlit instant
When the crumbling house would obliterate
Every impression of my sunlit life
In one image of final horror
Covering me with irrecoverable doom.

But the pulsation passed, and glass lay round me.
I rose from acrid dust, and in the night
I walked through clattering houses,
A prophet seeking tongues of flame.

Against a background of cloud, I saw
The houses kneel, exposed in their abject
Centennial selfish prayer: 'O Fate, this night
Save me from grief that punishes my neighbour!'
And the heads of all men living, cut open,
Would reveal the same shameless entreaty.

Then in the icy night, indifferent to our
Sulphurous nether fate, I saw
The dead of all time float on one calm tide
Among the foam of stars
Over the town, whose walls of brick and flesh
Are transitory dwellings
Of spirit journeying from birth to death.

The streets were filled with London prophets,
Saints of Covent Garden, Parliament Hill Fields,
Hampstead Heath, Lambeth and Saint Johns Wood
    Churchyard,
Who cried in cockney fanatic voices:
'In the midst of life is death!' And they all kneeled
And prayed against the misery manufactured
In mines and ships and mills, against
The greed of merchants, the vain hopes of churches,
And they played with children and marvelled at flowers,
And opened their low doors to invite in angels
Who had once climbed up sooty steeples
Like steeple jacks or chimney sweeps.

And they sang: 'We souls from the abyss,
Dancing in frozen peace of upper air,
Familiar with the fields of stars,
Say now: "Rejoice in the abyss!"
For hollow is the skull, the vacuum
Within the floating gold of Saint Paul's cross.
Unless your minds accept that emptiness
As the centre of your building and your love,
Under the bells of fox-gloves and of towers,
All human aims are stupefied denial
And each life feeds upon the grief of others
And the shamelessly entreating face
Of every man prays that he may be spared
Calamity that strikes each neighbouring face.'

A Man-made World

What a wild room
We enter, when the gloom
Of windowless night
Shuts us from the light

In a black, malicious box.
A freezing key locks
Us into utter dark
Where the nerves hark

For the man-made toys
To begin their noise.
The siren wails. After,
Broomsticks climb through air,

Then clocks burst through their springs,
Then the fire-bell rings.
Above and below comes
The anger of the drums.

Oh, what white rays gleaming
Against the sky's crouched ceiling!
What sudden flashes show
A woman who cries Oh!

In darkness where we are
With no saving star,
We hear the world we made
Pay back what we paid:

Money, steel, fire, stones,
Stripping flesh from bones,
With a wagging tongue of fear
Tormenting the ear,

Knocking at the outer skin,
To ask if any soul is in,
While the gloom descends
On our means become our ends.

The Conscript

On the turf's edge – grass flashing like a knife –
The conscript stands, above his native city.
He sees the sun's last rays consume that night
Whose tunnelled throat will swallow up the life
He's known – to thrust him on unknown tomorrow.
The sunset streaks the streets below with light.
He gazes on a red sky of self-pity
And sees his heart burn in a bowl of sorrow.

The action of tomorrow seems so real,
Necessity which will take him, so defined,
That this last night seems what he soon will feel,
Tomorrow's yesterday within his mind.
The setting sun belongs to a gold past
With the pathos of freedom left behind,
Discerned through blackening boughs of bitter contrast.

The hill grows pale, the strident colours fail,
An agate light encloses the home walls,
The gardens where his childhood played, are torn
Out of his eyes. Night's veil,
Dividing him from half his life, falls.

But then, beyond the rising star, appear
The armies marching to an earlier war.
The skeleton who strides last strikes the drum.
The conscript's soul is summoned to his eyes.
'Father!' he cries. 'Father! Father! I come!'

Almond Tree in a Bombed City

In the burned city, I see
The almond flower, as though
With great cathedral-fall

Barbarian rage set free
The angel of a fresco
From a cloister wall.

This flesh-petalled tree,
Angel of Fra Angelico,
With folded hands, bended knee
And arc of eloquent wing
(See the plumes like tongues grow
Promising the rainbow!),
To our world of ash will bring
Annunciation of Spring.

Responsibility: The Pilots Who Destroyed Germany, Spring 1945

I stood on a roof-top and they wove their cage,
Their murmuring, throbbing cage, in the air of blue
   crystal,
I saw them gleam above the town like diamond bolts
Conjoining invisible struts of wire,
Carrying through the sky their squadrons' cage
Woven by instincts delicate as a shoal of flashing fish.

They went. They left a silence in our streets below
Which boys gone to schoolroom leave in their play-ground:
A silence of asphalt, of privet hedge, of staring wall.
In the blue emptied sky their diamonds had scratched
Long curving finest whitest lines.
These the days soon melted into satin ribbons
Falling over heaven's terraces near the sun.

Oh, that April morning they carried my will
Exalted expanding singing in their aerial cage.
They carried my will. They dropped it on a German town.
My will exploded. Tall buildings fell down.

Then, when the ribbons faded, and the sky forgot,
And April was concerned with building nests and being hot
I began to remember the lost names and faces.

Now I tie the ribbons torn down from those terraces
Around the most hidden image in my lines,
And my life, which never paid the price of their wounds,
Turns thoughts over and over like a propeller,
Assumes their guilt, honours, repents, prays for them.

Tom's A-Cold

Such a day such a day when the rain
Makes sky and plain one dull pain

When noon is mirror of mud
And tonight will be moon of blood,

Such a day was the sum of my life
On this plain in this house with my wife

In this world where my charcoal days
Burned with a hidden blaze.

   I went clothed in herringbone tweed,
A grey shell, through which my bald head

Poked, like a nut, bare and lined.
My face was mask for my mind.

   I sat through the days as at table,
Pre-posthumously respectable,

And after dessert I could see
Time's worms turn and feed on me.

The intelligence gleamed in my eyes
Bright chips of fallen skies,

Whose grey vagueness recalled that joke
Old-world schoolchildren would poke

At me, as a boy: 'Tom's a poet,
Although, Tom, Tom, he don't know it.'

    Well, I used to ride on my bicycle
Down the country lanes, mile after mile,

And I'd think: 'How everything descends,
Clouds in the sky trailing dark horsetail ends,

'And at country fairs, the people with their hopes
Like puppets hung down from the sky on ropes

'By a time-machine which soon will jog them down
Two feet deep in mud of king and clown.'

    Forgive my old ways, but you come too late
To find my rhyming up-to-date,

Where your stilted galosh on grey mud squirms
Over me, at my feast of worms.

    Well, the others said: 'Life ascends, like a plant.'
But to me the sum of things seemed aslant,

Diagonal downward pressure of rain,
The waters driving under the plain.

Each dawn when I first opened eyelid
I seemed to lift a pyramid

Off appearances: this world seemed transparent
And, through its show, there were apparent

The folk reclining among roots
In villages under my boots.

    Through a looking glass I watched my uncouth
Skeleton starve on the bare truth.

A tumulus outlined the strata
Where flint-arrows pointed to data

Of those planned cities underground
Where the hierarchic bones are wound

In robes of rock, vaguening in shape
Back to that aristocrat, the ape.

For junketings, I entrained to the city
Where fogs pencilled humanity

Packed in penthouses, as in ships
Waiting at quay-side, till each slips

Out on the tide, bearing its cargo
Of passions to the world below.

The Red Light districts and the modish sins
Reminded me of animal skins,

Skin of snake, fur of cat, pelt of bear,
With the sense of eyes which had once looked there.

And I loved old attics where the lumber
Of past centuries seemed to slumber:

Faded silk, muslin pokes, hip baths, warming pans,
Rhinoceros horn, flint locks, armour, sedans,

Imagine the ladies and gentlemen
Of whose rolling souls these were the skin,
Chairs, beds, hats, clothes, they were snug in.

Shells and hides which left a trail
As over my grave, in his shell, sir, that snail.

Well, well, musing thus, it seemed incumbent
I should sympathise with the recumbent,

Who rolled in mud and clay of facts
And from flesh and blood moulded their acts.

I noted the wish of prostitutes
To sleep prematurely among roots,

I observed the baby's or the great lady's mouth
Tormented with desire as with drouth,

And the dark passions of the city
Wresting pleasure from steel reality,

Such I understood. I was there with all
Who thrust against life like a wall,

And who, in action and in thought,
Upon their harsh condition wrought

Some passionate image, to prove
Their naked need could shape their love.

I understood the sick botched lives,
The drink, the whoring and the knives.

   Well, what I abhorred were the great claims
Of inhuman superhuman aims

Attaching many to their gains
And making men links in their chains.

The wars, the abstract cause, false knowledge,
Exalting imperial privilege,

And in faith's name, the dubious creed
Usurping the single human need

Of knowing that we nothing know
Of whence we come and where we go

And nothing have, except we can
Comfort that poor condition, man.

   They called me pessimist in my day
Yet perhaps I was happier than they,

Living in life as in the hollow
Earth which I now lie below.

Within life always, as in the bone,
Part of all life, and thus alone.

I was imprisoned in each feature
Like nature whistling within nature,

The individual universal
Spirit shut in the animal.

I dwelt within my hollow minute
Like the song within the flute,

And where the song breathed through the hole
You may call, if you like, my soul:

That prince shut in a lonely tower
Robbed of hereditary power.

Now where I lie in gravestone rhyme,
My eyes are these two pools which climb

Through grey reflections to the sky –
My world asking your world: 'Why?'

Word

The word bites like a fish.
Shall I throw it back free
Arrowing to that sea
Where thoughts lash tail and fin?
Or shall I pull it in
To rhyme upon a dish?

Empty House

Then, when the child was gone,
I was alone
In the house, suddenly grown huge. Each noise
Explained its cause away,
Animal, vegetable, mineral,

Nail, creaking board, or mouse.
But mostly there was quiet of after battle
Where round the room still lay
The soldiers and the paintbox, all the toys.
    Then, when I went to tidy these away,
My hands refused to serve:
My body was the house,
And everything he'd touched, an exposed nerve.

Madonna

Below the scallop shell
Of the fanned sky
The clear girl is seated.
Her eyes are flowers
Thought by her body.
Her flesh a cloud
Edged with gold by her son.

The life in her life
Crouching to be born
Is head-downwards
In a lower room.
Inner flesh of peace
Withdrawn in a world
Where love makes the Real,
While the abstract Furies
Hunt the cities outside.

Her clear gaze divides
The world into two worlds:
Of kings who bring myrrh
To worship this birth:
Of heroes whose rays
Murder in the womb
Prenatal generations

Of reincarnate earth.
Her son will say: Choose!

Epithalamion

If my will could become this night
With all my conscious stars to witness
The marriage of this human pair –
Their fitness
The majesty upon my air –

And canopied beneath my trees
Their limbs on moss among my flowers –
My whisper of blessings and sighs
Would conspire with their own powers
Their furthest love to realize.

That they who in passionate meeting
Physically interpenetrate,
Should have my universe as bed
To lie down early there and late
By close and remote days re-wed.

That their explored happiness
Of mingled far discourse, should be
Stretched beyond this sheeted space
Where their curling limbs agree,
Into a timeless bodiless grace.

When them the hiding seas divide,
That their invisible presences
Should mingle between land and land:
All separating differences
Should be their hand reaching their hand.

Within this dragon-haunted era,
Let these two their faith perfect
To dome within their meeting mind

One clear sky of the intellect
Which no ill fate can make unkind.

O flesh and spirit of charity
Hammer that ring from their fused minute
Moulten where they are, part to part,
Whose circle appears absolute
And of the pure gold of the heart.

But I am not this night, I am
Only their well-wishing friend.
So, like this night, light by light,
I bring my presence to an end
With thoughts which are invisible
To make their loving possible.

O love, be indivisible!

Memento

Remember the blackness of that flesh
Tarring the bones with a thin varnish
Belsen Theresienstadt Buchenwald where
Faces were clenched fists of prayer
Knocking at the bird-song-fretted air.
Their eyes sunk jellied in their holes
Were held toward the sun like begging bowls
Their hands like rakes with fingernails of rust
Scratched for kindness from a little dust.
To many, in its beak no dove brought answer.

Speaking to the Dead in the Language of the Dead

I

So this young man reeled out
Of gambling den or brothel –

255

                         his face white
His hair ebony –
                    his waistcoat
Embroidered with small roses among stains
Of wine –

He drove into the night –
Hooves cannoned snow to moonlit smoke –
Black buttocks tossed under the sparkling bells –

Remote childhood towers mourned his life

Pursuit of happiness had exploded
A mine within his mind.

The lamentable word AGAIN
Exploded in his brain.

    II

        He ran past stone dogs of the palace gate
Up arching stairways aching like his head
Into his room –
                    flung himself down
His world revolving –
                        on his bed.

Then, through the darkness, images
Fixed into angels and devils of his pages.

'Again,' he sighed, 'Again.'

    III

Within that darkness where I see his room
    – Floor of black flame, star-pointed ceiling –
Within this midnight and beyond his tomb,
    He incised with a quill his vein of feeling
And wound the thin red blood out through the gloom
    To set down here for us: revealing

The dancer, his despair, at which we look –
His blood behind the white mask of his book.

Passion of women, flushed from his embracing,
    He dipped his pen in: his great night-limbed lovers
In operative moments of enlacing
    Were experiments in sensuous manoeuvres
From which he formed those tears and blushes gracing
    Today's libraries: and that sigh, which hovers
Through spaces between letters, white and far,
Is on his page the print of what we are.

His moon, *his* nightingale, torn from his time,
    Her tear, falling down centuries, hour by hour,
Her letter, weeping her wish through his rhyme,
    Her footstep, immanent: from such, his tower
Whose base stands in depraved quicklime,
    But whose high gleam reintegrates the flower,
Petal by petal, of time-outworn fashion,
In omnipresent coexistent passion.

It was enough for him that what is, is,
    To cut his jewels on time like jewels in clocks.
The tears, the diamonds, duels, moons, the kisses,
    He shut within his stanzas' iron locks
For us to look at. What was, what lived, is his
    Ecstasy. Marriage, ennui, pox,
And passion's disenchantment were unreal.
    His life was the bright cutting edge we feel.

Enough to praise it all. To burn! To live!
    Dip women, cards, remorse, and hell-rake fires,
In the poetical preservative!
    Brush all the nightingales to wires
Strung on the trees, behind a sigh! Oh give
    The ultimate affirmation when the choirs
Mass onto silence. Beyond ultimate harm
End with that opening 'O'! Death, like a charm!

IV

How is it
Your songs have sails which glide through death
And your transfigured head
Bends back futures to obeisant waves,
And your name like a deck as fresh as paint
Bridges that crowded hold
Loaded with ore of still-impassioned days
Fulgurant through our limbs? And you
Sail into our world yet still are you,
Blotches deleted from your brow
Where now the laurel scarcely dares
Bruise with praise the skin,
And future ages trembling here
Have thoughts like footprints across snow?

V

Perhaps we live in time as on a plain
Where our life is the blurred and jagged edge
Of all who ever died. We who are here
Fight out the fierce obsession of our wills
Upon each other's lives. Our violence
Enslaves our knowledge to our ignorance.

Yet in our feeling darkness, we are near
The sculptural presence of an influence
From the perfecting dead. Their night
Is words and statues and our light.
As though to live were to be doomfully blind
While the dead work within our living mind
Their art of chiaroscuro,
Using our darkness that they may grow clear.

Here on our edge of clamant inexperience
We use for murder our creating powers,
And, building, destroy spiritual towers.

Yet under blood and mire upon our hands
The dead move through us into ordered lands.

You who once wandered through this maze of being
We suffer now we are, become all you
Quickening through the darkness of our seeing,
More than you lived. Through us the true
Is purged of pitiless irrelevance
Where on our harsh edge of existence
You gain your quiet and white significance.

Through us you enter into your ideal,
Through us the formless dream becomes the real,
Our life bears your death-purified statue
Within this restless world you also knew.

We Cannot Hold onto the World

We cannot hold onto the world
However much we would
We stand on a turning wheel and are hurled
Beyond evil and good.

That running boy with mouth raised up
As though to kiss the winning cup –
Chest, flying buttress of the tape –
Eyes like thrown stars: lies on the ground
His fires drawn out with no sound
Through the narrow bullet wound.

That woman like a Muse, whose gaze
Stared through her contemporaries
Lighting their thoughts on floors of seas:
Filled her dress with large stones
And lay beneath an icy brook
Her beautiful eyes broken
Her mind unstrung – a mirror of unspoken

Thoughts (white now as her bones)
Pages of an unwritten book.

A turning wheel scatters
Stars upon the wind.
Who shall regain
The concentrated mind
From blowing dust outside, and seas, and driving rain?

Time in Our Time

Moving upwards through space, heaped with Now,
O self of each phenomenal instant,
Moving from inconceivable beginning
To inconceivable end–
                    Upon Time,
I was cast naked out of non-existence,
Upon this stair climbing between the stars,
Lifted some steps on Time,
Soon to reject me, thrown-down card,
Cadaver planing and spiralling through dark,
Dissolving into dust, dissolving into space.

Tomorrow and yesterday are pictures
Remembered and foreseen, painted within
Man's two profiles facing Past and Future, pivoted
On the irreducible secret diamond
His Now. Past and Future, pictures only,
And all events and places distant from
The instant of perception in the brain,
Are memories and prophecies.
All distant times and places, all events
In other minds, all knowledge folded
In books, Pasts petrified in statues,
Spatial distances witnessed by telescopes,

Prehuman histories embossed on fossils,
Silent messages from star to star,
Exist only in the flash within the single flesh.

Yet some Pasts do persist within the Now,
Within the Now some Futures lift
Witnessing trumpets blowing prophecies
Of stones which will bud into cities.
The snow-white Acropolis collects
Many eyes of dead Greeks from far histories
Held now in living eyes. It is
A column through Time, stone doves ascending
A prayer of skies, a ring of changes
Reintegrating each instant into Athens.

Oh save me in this day, when Now
Is a towering pillar of dust which sucks
The ruin of a world into its column.
When to perceive is to be part of that cloud
Whose castle changes into dragon.
Oh, though the Past dissolve, may all that was
Once idea integrated into stone
Enter my secret mind at the whirling centre
Of the external storm: and combine with
A love which penetrates through falling flesh
To paint the image in my heart
Of that past greatness and that once-willed Future,
Beyond the storm, which still can make a world.

1949–1970

Travelling Northwards Home

From the red peaks like roots dried up in air
Worn by gales and years to fruitless stone,
With sides parched gold by killing suns;

From heat twisting through white dust like snakes,
From skies hammering mountains and sea
Into one cracked and violet crystal.

To me travelling Northwards home, suddenly green
Blazed, from grass and barley fields
Along rivers where there were flowering trees;

And like a liquid trail of fire was the mile-long mildness
Which I had never looked at until this,
When being restored to me, it seemed visible happiness.

[1949]

Terza Rima

From the German of Hugo Von Hofmannsthal

And still I feel their breath upon my cheek!
How can it be that these days, not yet distant
Are gone, quite gone, and never will come back?

This is a thing none knows well how to say
And far too terrible for our lament:
That everything glides past and runs away

And my own I, which is hemmed in by nothing,
Slipped over from a little child this way
To me like a dog, strange, dumb and foreign.

Then: that a century past I still was here
And my forebears, in winding sheets, are kin
And part of me as much as my own hair,

Are as much one with me as my own hair.

[1950]

Ballad of the Exterior Life

From the German of Hugo Von Hofmannsthal

And children grow up with their deep-eyed gaze
Who know of nothing, they grow up and die,
And all mankind continue on their ways.

And from the bitter the sweet fruits grow high
And in the night they fall down like dead birds
And lie there a few days and putrefy.

And the wind ever blows and many words
Are said by us, who learn ever anew,
And we taste joy and limbs becoming tired.

And streets run through the grass and places show
Here and there, with torches, a pond, trees,
And menacing, and deathly-withered too . . .

Wherefore were they built up? And why are these
Never alike? And are too many to name?
What takes the place of laughter, tears, disease?

What use all this to us, and all this game
Of growing old and ever being alone
And wandering never seeking any aim?

What use of such things to have seen so many?
Yet much is said by him who 'evening' says
A word from which deep meaning and grief run
As from the hollow comb the heavy honey.

[1951]

In Attica

Again, again, I see this form repeated:
The bare shadow of a rock outlined
Against the sky; declining gently to
An elbow; then the scooped descent
From the elbow to the wrist of a hand that rests
On the plain.
                              Again, again,
That arm outstretched from the high shoulder
And leaning on the land.
                              As though the torsoed
Gods, with heads and lower limbs broken off,
Plunged in the sky, or buried under earth,
Had yet left arms extended here as pointers
Between the sun and plain:
                              had made this landscape
Human, like Greek steles, where the dying
Are changed to stone on a gesture of curved air,
Lingering in their infinite departure.

[1952]

Messenger

(*To Georges Seferis*)

O messenger, held back
From your journey! – Walled in,
Imagination trails leaves
Shut from the sun!

＊

In what cellar of his brain
A map flashes with
The island-sprinkled sea, and

Mountain-vertebrate land
– Osseous hand
Whose fingers spread
Peninsulas. His eyes
Cut the day
Out of sunlight all day,
Diamonds of the light,
Shed on agate hills
Their gleams all night.

Upon one headland
Marble foot treads.
Sunium. Columns at edge
Of keel-scarred Aegean.
His hot will races
Through brake and flint.
Anemone, rock rose,
Asphodel, thyme,
Tear his thighs with love.
To the temple he runs
And kisses the white stone.

Before he can
Say what he can,
He lifts his eyes where
Grooved columns are quivers
From which the archer sun
Takes arrows he shoots
Through his eye-sockets.

Above the temple rooflessness,
Clouds are a roof
Remembering lines
Of a frieze whose procession
Fell out of the sky.
On a wave of the air
Hands, simple as light,

Bent. Their tunics
Were marble breeze.
Embossed hooves
Of quadruple quadrupeds
Oxen and horses,
Stamped. Manes were crests
Of torches which burned
Through nostrils hewn like eyes.

A clear chisel cut
These lines taut as knots
Which yet have the freedom
To un-knot hearts.
The raised hand of a god
Has blood through veins where
The human flows into
The absolute.

What message could speak
From the new ruined Europe
To the old, ruined Greece?
None! Yet believe in
Words where worlds cross
Where all that is not
Must swear: 'I am!'

[1953]

To My Daughter

Bright clasp of her whole hand around my finger,
My daughter, as we walk together now,
All my life I'll feel a ring invisibly
Circle this bone with shining: when she is grown
Far from today as her eyes are far already.

[1953]

Missing My Daughter

This wall-paper has lines that rise
Upright like bars, and overhead,
The ceiling's patterned with red roses.
On the wall opposite the bed
The staring looking-glass encloses
Six roses in its white of eyes.

Here at my desk, with note-book open
Missing my daughter, makes those bars
Draw their lines upward through my mind.
This blank page stares at me like glass
Where stared-at roses wish to pass
Through petalling of my pen.

An hour ago, there came an image
Of a beast that pressed its muzzle
Between bars. Next, through tick and tock
Of the reiterating clock
A second glared with the wide dazzle
Of deserts. The door, in a green mirage,

Opened. In my daughter came.
Her eyes were wide as those she has,
The round gaze of her childhood was
White as the distance in the glass
Or on a white page, a white poem.
The roses raced around her name.

   [1953]

Nocturne

Their six-weeks-old daughter lies
in her cot, crying out the night. Their hearts
Are sprung like armies, waiting

270

To cross the gap to where her loneliness
Lies infinite between them. This child's cry
Sends rays of a star's pain through endless dark;
And the sole purpose of their loving
Is to disprove her demonstration
Of all love's aidlessness. Words unspoken
Out of her mouth unsaying, prove unhappiness
Pure as innocence, virgin of tragedy,
Unknowing reason. Star on star of pain
Surround her cry to make a constellation
Where human tears of victims are the same
As griefs of the unconscious animals.

Listening, the parents know this primal cry
Out of the gates of life, hollows such emptiness,
It proves that all men's aims should be, all times,
To fill the gap of pain with consolation
Poured from the mountain-sided adult lives
Whose minds like peaks attain to heights of snow:
The snow should stoop to wash away such grief.
Unceasing love should lave the feet of victims.

Yet, when they lift their heads out of such truths,
Today mocks at their prayers. To think this even
Suffices to remind them of far worse
Man-made man-destroying ills which threaten
While they try to lull a child. For she
Who cries for milk, for rocking, and a shawl,
Is also subject to the rage of causes
Dividing peoples. Even at this moment
Eyes might fly between them and the moon,
And a hand touch a lever to let fall
That which would make the street of begging roofs
Pulverize and creep skywards in a tower:
Down would fall baby, cradle, and them all.

That which sent out the pilot to destroy them
Was the same will as that with which they send

An enemy to kill their enemy. Even in this love
Running in shoals on each side of her bed,
Is fear, and hate. If they shift their glances
From her who weeps, their eyes meet other eyes
Willed with death, also theirs. All would destroy
New-born, innocent streets. Necessity,
With abstract head and searing feet, men's god
Unseeing the poor amulets of flesh,
Unhearing the minutiae of prayer.

   Parents like mountains watching above their child,
Envallied here beneath them, also hold
Upon their frozen heights, the will that sends
Destruction into centres of the stones
Which concentrated locked centennial stillness
For human generations to indwell.

   Hearing their daughter's cry which is the speech
Of indistinguishable primal life,
They know the dark is filled with means which are
Men's plots to murder children. They know too
No cause is just unless it guards the innocent
As sacred trust: no truth but that
Which reckons this child's tears an argument.

   [1953]

Dylan Thomas

   (*November* 1953)

In November of Catherine Wheels and rockets
This roaring ranter, man and boy,
Proved Guy Fawkes true, and burned on a real fire.
His rhymes that stuffed his body were the straw,
His poems he shed out of his pockets,
Were squibs and sweets and string and wire,
The crackling gorse thorn crowned him with spiked joy.

Where he sang, burning, round his neck a cup
Begged: 'Pennies, pennies, for the Guy!'
And every coin from every passer by
When it was melted, he drank fiery up.
And all his sins, before his voice that spoke,
Shot angels skywards. Now, that he should die
Proves the fire was the centre of his joke.

[1953]

Sirmione Peninsula

Places I shared with her, things that she touched –
Could I ever have known
How untouchable these would become
The day after she was gone?

Sirmio's peninsula stretches out into the lake
Like one spoke thrusting to the centre
Of the mountain-circled water: where
I stand now, through brush-branched olive trees
And ragged broken arches
Ancient Romans built so long ago,
I see the water's bowl-edge round me, in an almost perfect O.

This I saw once before, with her, as long it seems now,
As though I were one of those Romans. I noticed then
The wings of the water flashing through torn-brick arches
The olive leaves turned by the sky from silver to blue
The lizards like shocks through the grass,
The mountains ringed glassily round the lake, seeming
Gray dolphins painted on glass.

I watched and watched then as I watch and watch now. And
   she who was with me seemed sad
Seeing me self-enclosed in my view of the view
That shut her out from me, as though at my desk in my room,
In the midst of our Lake Garda honeymoon.

Now the mountains might fall and crush me. All the wide rim
Of their up-diving shapes from the water, brings pain
Of unapproachable things
Making me conscious that I am unseeing alone
Since she with whom I would be is not by my side
With her hair blown back by the winds of the whole lake view,
Lips parted as though to greet the flight of a bird.

[1954]

Critic in the Spring-time

PROLOGUE

'Hail, *Sagittarius, Muse* – of *Critic*'s world!'
    Her I salute, where, with great lead wings furled,
She stands. Behind her, ten distorting bows
And twice as many of her blunted arrows.
In her rapt eyes I see revolve that dream,
'Britain is always wrong,' which is her theme.
    Strapping, and strapped in ideologic boots,
She always misses, but she always shoots.
Week after week, weak rhymes dart from her pen,
Dynamite of *New Statesman* stateswomen.
    O *Sagittarius*, aid me now! I sing
That day when *Critic* 'notices' the Spring.
Of all Black Fridays in Great Turnstile's year
This, this, ah, this, is far the worst to bear.
    One shrub has thrust out of steel buds that harden
In the perennial Winter of his garden,
Two petals! *London Diary* readers know
The Ineluctable fated to follow.
    A morose joy will soon suffuse his 'column':
In *Critic* gay, we recognize – the Solemn.
His pen – remorseless Tragedy's machine –
Will sketch him Hero on his village green.

274

Now Five dread Acts of freezing levity
Will purge the reader, with Terror and Pity.

The Curtain – like him – Rises. Up, with dawn!
His typographic toes impress his lawn,
His pen he loads for Action: interview
With *Park*, his gardener, in the printless dew.
    SUN, behold *Park*, who now unshaved, appears.
Which are his ribs? Which is his rake? What years
Heaped such white havoc? Nothing, but the toil
Of vainly raking *Critic*'s fruitless soil.
    CRITIC: 'Good *Park*, see your replies are true
To this examination set for you.
Hide nothing! Have you ever known a year
Windier than this? To print the Truth, we dare!
Tell me the worst! That's what I'm used to hear!'
    Less with his voice, than with his chattering bones,
The Ancient croaks above *Critic*'s bass groans:
'It stand to reason, zur, since old Windmill
Were done away with, Wind can work his will
Wi' nowt to stop him where they tore a hole.
Wi'out Windmill, Wind gets out o' control.'
'Thank you, Good *Park*. It weighed upon my mind.
– That Weathercock, veered by each toughest Wind.'
    They talk of tempests. Syllables from *Park*
Critic takes down. He notes well! Each remark
(He knows) through *London Diary*'s gloom will spark
Against that foil of uncontrasting dark.
For, there, all's one 'Pea Souper,' and the slow
Ideas, like cars through fog-bound traffic go,
Where asterisks their Belisha Beacons show.

    *

Poor *Park*! *Fool* to this *Lear*, playing Prelude
To *Horror* which now breaks loose, wild and crude.
Reader, prepare for scenes of Turpitude.

ACT TWO: SCENE, *Critic in the Village Pub.*

(If even in London, in the S—e Club,
His gorgon powers of turning men to stone
Through nothing but embarrassment, are known,
What chance have Essex yokels? Answer – None.
– Stalagmites, petrified amidst their fun!
(*This* ACT's *too realistic to be done.*)

ACT THREE

Oh, better to be petrified, than be
Reincarnated to live through ACT THREE.
These, part-lapidified, he now revives
To face that devilish game on which he thrives,
Horror's worst horror. Reader – you know – he
Has grim work still to do: *Shove-Halfpenny*!
    See yon rough yokel drag the reluctant coin
Out of his pocket (clutched against his groin)
And yield it to the board. Triumphantly,
Critic swoops down, all his ten thumbs afly.
Halfpennies, from ten directions, strike the floor.
Critic collects them, counts: 'One! Two! Three! Four!'
Then bangs the board and roars amain: 'More! More!'

ACT FOUR

(*Critic*, off-stage. As Bradley points out in
Shakespearean Tragedy, often throughout Fourth
Acts heroes are conspicuous for their absence.)

He's gone! Defrosted spirits thaw and rise
Like mercury in thermometric eyes.
The liquor which his gaze had disintoxicated

Now re-ferments, and flickers flame, elated.
Out of his barrel-top, poor 'repressed' Beer's
Humpty-Dumpty-bright frothed head appears.

So, *Critic* gone, everyone has one on
Everyone, and everyone's thoughts run on
Him what's just left, phenomenon from Lunnon.

'What was HE like?' – 'Like No-one no-one know.'
'The body, an agnostic preaching scarecrow.'
'The hair, where some sad jackdaw built her nest.'
'Poor soul! His laugh alone made me depressed.'
'Sure, he's some *Hamlet* of the village scene
Arts Council sent here. We shall blush unseen.'
'I know,' a sweet voice thrills, ''tis some great lord,
'A Royal Duke at least.' 'I'll wage my word
That through yon veins flows aristocratic blood.
He visits Essex when it suits his mood.
He has such whims. He is some great Eccentric.'

Thus Legend weaves its wondrous web round *Critic*.

ACT FIVE

But where is he? Transfigured Night has drawn
Curtains across that frightful stage, his lawn.
Oh, hush! *Park*'s potting shed the place is
Where *Critic* is encircled by Three Graces –
Dorothy, *Doreen*, *Sagittarius*,
Immense, intense, and, like Himself, so serious.

See *Sagittarius*! She's trying to fix
Her sharpened yet unsharpened twisted sticks,
Pointed, and pointless, like their politics.

O *Sagittarius*, ever pointing higher,
Sometimes thy arrows, like pianoforte wire,
Fall back, entangling her who is their firer.

Yet well she loves this life of paradox!
A far, far, better thing than darning socks.
She wears the trousers, and his snooks she cocks!

See *Dorothy* and *Doreen*! Both are dressed
In anyone else's worst, which is their best.
Their smiles beam Eastwards, and their sneers go West.
   Two zips enseal them, one front, one behind,
Their foreheads' frown zips up their single mind.
   Not monsoon rainier, nor typhoon windier,
Than this their *Dirge*, '*SET WET*' to reach till *India*:
   'Dance hand in hand round *Critic* all night long
   And sing that *Critic* never never never never can do
     wrong!'

  [1954]

One

Here then
She lies
Her hair a scroll along
The grooved warm nape
Her lips half-meeting on a smile
Breath almost unbreathing
O life
A word this word my love upon the white
Linen
As though I wrote her name out on this page.

My concentration on her quietness
Intensifies like light ringed from this lamp
That throws its halo upward on the ceiling

Here we
Are one
Here where my waking walks upon her sleep
One within one
And darkly meeting in the hidden child.

  [1954]

Dog Rose

Dog rose, unruffling petals
Transparent pink within blue transparent,
Blowing scent faint as pink
Blowing scent light as blue,

Across how many fields you call me back
Back to the small days of small hands
Rolling tight fists of saw-edged leaves
To mix the smell of briar with their own sweat.

Your hedges I saw anchored
On fields where they dropped thorn-hook lines
In glassy seas of grass;

Your flowers were ruffling faces
Of little princes open for one day
On leaf-thick summer:

All washed in white-rime morning
All crowned with pollen noon
All folded prayer at dusk

                                    cut down
By the brief axe of the Tower night
That lopped off many nodding heads of princes.

  [1954]

To Samuel Barber

No conductor with his wand
Can reverse the tempo, and
Bring back that distant day upon
Which, in 1937, London,
I listened to you sing your music.
In all the streets there is no physic

279

To question what the windows say:
'Both your heads have turned quite gray.'

'I was' lies within 'I am'
That you were Sam is to be Sam.
'We were' 'we shall be' says 'we are'
However past, however future.
In your music, in my books,
We both are being, if each looks.

[1957]

Orpheus: Adam: Christ

He who sings most sweetly is the one who listens.
Orpheus in the branches of the world a tree

Enchanted animals: but they had first enthralled him
– Swayed through his blood their rhythm he made music.

The sun hewed out his eyes; birds whistled through his bones:
From both he made the tunes to freeze them on his flute.

Before this, Adam was axle of Creation,
The hub of spoked unicorns wheeling round him.

Spitted on animal fire, he suffered beasts their names
And gardened life in Eden with magic tongue.

Then Christ, nailed to his Cross, received into his wounds
Bitter cup of curses men poured through them –

Eli eli lama sabachthani. This he changed – like
Orpheus taming spirits, Adam naming beasts –

To christening mankind bound here by endless love
Through agony transformed to joyous Hymn.

[1958]

Subject: Object: Sentence

A subject thought, because he had a verb
With several objects, that he ruled a sentence.
Had not Grammar willed to him substantives
Which he came into, as his just inheritance?

His objects were *wine, women, wealth*,
A whole subordinate clause – *all life can give*.
He grew so fond of having these that, finally,
He found himself becoming too subjective.

Subject, the dictionary warned, means *being ruled by
Person or thing*. Was he not passion's slave?
To achieve detachment, he must be objective
Which meant to free himself from the verb *have*.

Seeking detachment, he studied the context
Around his sentence, to place it in perspective:
Then parsed it, made a critical analysis,
And then re-read it, feeling more objective.

Then, with a shock, he realized that *sentence*
Like *subject-object* is treacherously double.
A *sentence* is condemned to stay as written –
As in *life-* or *death-sentence*, for example.

[1958]

Instructions

First. You have to follow
A thread that leads you through
A labyrinth of streets
Staring at you from windows
Howling at you from cars.
       But do not imagine

At the centre, a square,
Roofed over, shut in on all sides,
A Way In but no *Way Out*,
Bellowing only with minotaur.
Minotaur is everywhere.
Minotaur is in your head.

Next. Hold tight to the thread
In your hand. But do not imagine
At last it leads up
Into all light outside.
Is it not already white?
Or – look again – perhaps red?
White and red. Intertwining
Streets in your head
With all light outside.
It is all you will get!

Next. When what will seem to you night,
Finally blots out your sight
Then you'll explode.
Turned inside out
You'll show I AM for all to read.
Perhaps *I AM all light outside*
Perhaps *I AM the streets in the head*
Minotaur roaring through
Labyrinth, again and again.

Do not imagine, though,
Whatever may be decided,
That you will ever know!

   [1958]

Journal Leaves

I DREAM NO DREAM

His dream surely no dream but his real future
Was this: his body lay stretched on his bed
Hovering above which his senses had worked loose.
Sight, without eyes, above him, looking down
Saw white and brittle shells lodged in his knees.
And touch, worked separate, without hands, could feel
Shells and bones together involuted.

  Waking, he sought to trace that nightmare's meaning
To some inverted willing. Incontrovertibly
The answer came though that, as the drowned past
Has cast cockles inland from days when this
Was once the ocean bed, there is a future
To which our bones already are the past.
And consciousness sways over shells and bones
Which are the last grave in the dreamer's mind.

II LOTHAR

In 1929 we drove out to
The marshlands, where the thatched roofs make
Nests, under nests of storks.
In the artist's white new house we lay
On mats where the June evening
Poured in one line of Mozart through a flute.
Lothar lit a log fire in the yard
And Irma came out on the balcony
Gown billowing round the unborn child.
Sparks, floating up in flakes around her skirt,
Made golden brooches of her eyes. Lothar said
That while the child was being born he'd take
His bicycle and ride on dusty roads
Flat all the way to Holland.

Pedalling unendingly leaning over
The handlebars, his boxy head thrust forward
From which the blonde hair jutted back: and in his eyes
That prairie look reflected from the fire.

[1962]

'Earth-treading Stars that Make Dark Heaven Light'

How can they call this dark when stars
That all day long the sun rules out
Show brilliant at the ends of space?
Journeying down centennial rays
These antique worlds stand in Earth's air –
The coruscating helmets of
Warriors born before the births
Of Greeks who chose their diamond names.

All day the sun paints surfaces,
Commander of dial hands, pursues
The flying instants of last fashion.
But when night comes and windows hew
Gold oblongs out of distances
Of solid sky, the park becomes
The fulgurous centre of the city
Drawing from lonely streets the lonely

Under its boughs. There, in each other,
Beyond their coverings of clothes
And names, they see flesh blaze, and then
Those pasts they were before they were
Themselves, emerge: ape, lion, fox. Their mouths
Conjoined, they utter cries that once
Jibbered upside down through branches
Before woods ever dreamed of huts.

But two there are who look so deep
Into each other's night, they see
Yet further than their meeting bodies
And earliest most brilliant star,
To where is nothing but a vow
That is their truth. Those instruments
Of world made flesh, they bore to prove
Before all change, their changeless word.

[1965]

Middle East

One morning, between journeys, rising
From bed at an inn, I went out.
Half an hour after dawn
Already the sun had cut

Night – one shadow – into many
Shadows dissecting day – one light –
Into white squares white oblongs.
Palm trees were dull, figs electrically bright.

Downhill, tangled wires criss-crossed
Between roofs. At the street's end
Beyond corners like prows. I saw
The Mediterranean extend

Its line of absolute horizon
From which hung the sea, royal as clover.
Waves flashed lights through air
Pointillist as pollen all over.

I ran down the street past bicycles, donkeys,
Jangling, shouting, robed, turbaned crowd;
Past hollows of deep entrances
Through which rugs, copper, oranges glowed;

Past slaughtered cadavers
Of sheep and goat, hanging from hooks;
Succulent sweets fly-preempted,
Communist pamphlets, pornographic books;

Till I'd descended to the ocean
Sliding parallelograms multilinear.
On the far shore, distant mountains
Curving like dolphins, rose clear.

Skeletal boys, pharaonically sculptured,
Stretched out rods from rocks, in wait
For fish, whose ancestors, stupid as these,
Took Cleopatra's bait.

And the sun, pompous as God,
Sat enthroned in his central sky: to prove
He still melts unhygienic passions
In his furnace of hygienic love.

[1969]

Diary Poems

26 JANUARY 1970

November, Auden came to stay in London.
Famous, much-photographed creased face
Netted in the past, his eyes can only tell
Their solitude. His talk
Is concentrated 'I', 'I get up at eight,
Then I have cawfee and rolls, then I do
The Times Crossword, if I can get *The Times*.
Then I go to the john, and then I work
Until elevenses, when I have tea.
I have to have lunch at one precisely.
At six precisely I fix up Martinis

90 per cent vodka 70 proof.
Dinner at 7.30 not one moment later
Or I tend to become repetitive.
Then at nine byebyes like mother taught me.
Oh! the relief of getting between the sheets!'

'How should I educate my 4-year-old son?'
Marianne asks. He hoists his face towards her
Then blandly says: 'Send him to boarding school
As soon as he's 7. That's what happened with me.
Teach him Latin. If he makes a false quantity
Beat him like I was beaten if I did.' She tells him
Of her suicide attempt. 'I took a hundred tablets
In Sydney.' 'Now that's naughty.
I take one every night
For sleeping and a Benzedrine each morning
For working.' He clicks his mouth shut.
I say: 'You talk of nothing but yourself.'
He looks full at me with a kind of sweetness
And says: 'What else should I talk about then?
What else do I know about?' Now Chris produces
A magazine called *Suck*. 'Will you autograph this, please, sir?
Your wonderful poem called "The Platonic Blow Job".'
'I wrote that as an exercise in scazons.'
They smile. He can say what he likes, they know
He has written the sexiest beautifullest openest
Poem about a pick-up in Greenwich Village
The knock-out that makes all their sex soap-opera.
Back home, he says to me: 'Promise me one thing,
Promise me this one thing, you'll never
However she may ask you, show to Lizzie
That poem.' Under the net of lines, he smiles
Under the lines the heart ever the same.

I had been in Florence on 2 January when our granddaughter
Saskia was born in a hospital there.

We looked at Matthew's child, our granddaughter,
Through the glass screen, where eight babies
Blazed like red candles on a table.
Her crumpled face and hands were like
Chrysalis and ferns uncurling.
'Is our baby a genius?' he asked a nun.
We went to the Uffizi and he looked at
Italian Primitives, and found
All of their Christ-childs ugly.
He started drawing Maro and her daughter
Nine hours after Saskia had been born.

28 FEBRUARY 1970

I drove to New York and dined with Auden. My sixty-first
birthday: his sixty-third was two days ago, 26 February.

Dined with Auden. He'd been at Milwaukee
Three days, talking to the students.
'They loved me. They were entranced.' His face lit up
   the scene.
I saw there the picture of him, crammed into
Carpet-bag clothes and carpet slippers,
His face alone alive alone above them.
He must have negotiated himself into the room
Like an object, a prize, a gift that knows its worth,
Measuring his value out to them on scales
Word weighed by word, absorbed in his own voice.
He knows they're young, and, better, that he's old.
He shares his distance from them like a joke.
They love him for it. This, because they feel

That he belongs to none yet gives to all.
They see him as an object, artefact, that time
Has ploughed criss-cross with all these lines
Yet has a core within that purely burns.

THE GENEROUS DAYS (1971)

To Matthew, Maro and Saskia
con amore

If It Were Not

If it were not for that
Lean executioner, who stands
Ever beyond a door
With axe raised in both hands –

All my days here would be
One day – the same – the drops
Of light edgeless in light
That no circumference stops.

Mountain, star and flower
Single with my seeing
Would – gone from sight – draw back again
Each to its separate being.

Nor would I hoard against
The obliterating desert
Their petals of the crystal snow
Glittering on the heart.

My hand would never stir
To follow into stone
Hair the wind outlines on sky
A moment, and then gone.

What gives edge to remembering
Is death. It's that shows, curled,
Within each falling moment
An Antony, a world.

She came into the garden
And, walking through deep flowers, held up
Our child who, smiling down at her,
Clung to her throat, a cup.

Clocks notch such instances
On time: no time to keep

Beyond the eye's delight
The loss that makes it weep.

I chisel memories
Within a shadowy room,
Transmuting gleams of light to ships
Launched into a tomb.

Lost Days

(*To John Lehmann*)

Then, when an hour was twenty hours, he lay
Drowned under grass. He watched the carrier ant,
With mandibles as trolley, push in front
Wax-yellow specks across the parched cracked clay.

A tall sun made the stems down there transparent.
Moving, he saw the speedwell's sky blue eye
Start up next to his own, a chink of sky
Stamped deep through the tarpaulin of a tent.

He pressed his mouth against the rooted ground.
Held in his arms, he felt the earth spin round.

The Chalk Blue Butterfly

The Chalk Blue (clinging to
A harebell stem, where it loops
Its curving wirefine neck
From which there hangs the flowerbell
Shaken by the wind that shakes
Too, the butterfly) –
Opens now, now shuts, its wings,
Opening, shutting, on a hinge

Sprung at touch of sun or shadow.
   Open, the sunned wings mirror
Minute, double, all the sky.
   Shut, the ghostly underwing
Is cloud-opaque, bordered by
Copper spots embossed
By a pygmy hammering.

   I look and look, as though my eyes
Could hold the Chalk Blue in a vice,
Waiting for some other witness
– That child's blue gaze, miraculous.
But today I am alone.

Boy, Cat, Canary

Our whistling son called his canary Hector.
'Why?' I asked. 'Because I had always about me
More of Hector with his glittering helmet than
Achilles with his triple-thewed shield.' He let Hector
Out of his cage, fly up to the ceiling, perch on his chair, hop
Onto his table where the sword lay bright among books
While he sat in his yellow jersey, doing his homework.
Once, hearing a shout, I entered his room, saw what carnage:
The Siamese cat had worked his tigerish scene.
Hector lay on the floor of his door-open cage
Wings still fluttering, flattened against the sand.
Parallel, horizontal, on the rug, the boy lay
Mouth biting against it, fists hammering boards.
'Tomorrow, let him forget,' I prayed. 'Let him not see
What I see in this room of miniature Iliad –
The golden whistling howled down by the dark.'

A Father in Time of War

I

On a winter night I took her to the hospital.
Lying in bed, she clasped my hand
In her two hands. I watched the smile
Float on her pain-torn happy face –
Light stretched on the surface of a well
At the bottom of which, hidden from sight,
Curled a minute human phantom.

II

Next morning, I went to hospital
On a bus that drove through streets
Unwinding back to the First Day.
A solitary street cleaner
Hosed water over hopeless rubble.
In front of her charred and splintered door
A woman scrubbed
A doorstep whiter than her hair.
A ladder lifted up into the air
Arms that bore a minute human phantom.

III

Now we watch him lying in the grass
In the garden. His eyes
See branches sway. Birds fly forward
Against the backwards-flying clouds.
Brushing yellow flowers, green leaves, his eyes
Pout like his mouth across her breast:
Voluptuous wondering, drinking in
The dizzy spinning tilting upside-
down flags of the world new born.

Child Falling Asleep in Time of War

Smooth the sheet. Then kiss her forehead –
Bone shell the ocean dreams inside.
Dark is voyage. This bed, her boat
Drawn up on the incoming tide
One word, 'goodnight', will thrust afloat.

Sleeping, my child seems this calm air
That she smiles through. Her breathing is,
Moment to moment, star to star,
Measure of the measureless
Nature dreaming under war.

Almond Tree by a Bombed Church

(*For Henry Moore*)

Jewel-winged almond tree,
Alighting here on bended knee –
To the shattered street you bring
Annunciation of Spring –

Where, before, an angel was
That wrestled in the leaded glass,
Now, risen from the fallen window,
Leaves and burning petals glow.

Resurrected from the dust
Of bricks and rubble, blood and rust,
Luminous new life appears
On leaf and petal, trembling spears.

V.W. (1941)

That woman who, entering a room,
Stood, staring round at all, with rays
From her wild eyes, till people there
– And books, pictures, furniture –
Became transformed within her gaze
To rocks, fish, wrecks, Armada treasure –
Gold lit green on the sea floor –

Filled her dress with heavy stones
Then lay down in a shallow brook
Where a wave, like casing glass,
Curves over her shattered face,
And clothes – torn pages of her book –
Mad mind as cold and silent as the stones.

Mein Kind Kam Heim

(After Stephan George)

My boy came home
The seawind still curves through his hair –
His step still weighs
Fears withstood and young lust for adventure.

The saltbrine spray
Still brands the bronze bloom of his cheek:
Rind quickly ripened
In foreign suns bewildering haze and flame.

His glance is grave
Already with some secret hidden from me
And lightly veiled
Since from his Spring he to our winter came.

So sudden burst
This burgeoning that almost shy I watched

And forbade mine
His mouth that chose another mouth as kiss.

My arm surrounds
Him who unmoved from mine for other worlds
Blossoms and grows –
My one my own endlessly far from me.

Sleepless

Awake alone in the house
I heard a voice
– Ambiguous –
With nothing nice.

Perhaps knocking windows?
A board loose in the floor?
A gap where a draught blows
Under the door?

Repairs needed? Bills?
Is it owls hooting – pay! –
Or it might be the walls
Crumbling away

Reminding – 'You, too,
Disintegrate
With the plaster – but you
At a faster rate.'

Or it might be that friend once
I shut outside
Sink or swim – well, he sank –
In my sleep cried

'Let me in! Let me in!',
Tapping at the pane.
Him I imagine,
Twenty years in the rain.

The Generous Days

I

His are the generous days that balance
Soul and body. Should he hear the trumpet
Shout justice from a sky of ice
– Lightning through the marrow –
At once one with that cause, he'd throw
Himself across some far, sad parapet –
Soul fly up from body's sacrifice,
Immolated in the summons.

II

But his, too, are the days when should he greet
Her who goes walking, looking for a brooch
Under plantains at dusk beside the path,
And sidelong looks at him as though she thought
His glance might hide the gleam she sought –
He would run up to her, and each
Find the lost clasp hid in them both,
Mindless of soul, so their two bodies meet.

III

Body soul – soul body – are his breath
– Or light or shadow cast before his will –
In these, his generous days. They prove
His utmost being simply is to give.
Wholly to die, or wholly, else, to live!
If the cause ask for death, then let it kill.
If the blood ask for life, then let it love.
Giving is all to life or all to death.

After, of course, will come a time not this
When he'll be taken, stripped, strapped to a wheel
That is a world, and has the power to change
The brooch's gold, the trumpet's golden blaze
– The lightning through the blood those generous days –
Into what drives a system, like a fuel.
Then to himself he will seem loathed and strange,
Have thoughts still colder than the thing he is.

On the Photograph of a Friend, Dead

Dead friend, this picture proves there was an instant
That with a place – leaf-dazzling garden – crossed
When – mirror of midday – you sent
Shadow and light from living flesh into
The sensitive dark instrument

That snatched your image for its opposite
And, in a black cell, stood you on your head.
So, on the film, when I developed it,
Black showed white, where you had shadow, white
Black, where smiling up, your eyes were sunlit.

To me, under my hand, in the Dark Room
Laid in a bath of chemicals, your ghost
Emerged gelatinously from that tomb;
Looking-glass, soot-faced, values all reversed
The shadows brilliant and the lights one gloom.

Reverse of that reverse, your photograph
Now positively scans me with
Your quizzical ironic framed half-laugh.
Your gaze oblique under sun-sculptured lids
Endlessly asks me: 'Is this all we have?'

Voice from a Skull

(*Futami-ga-ura, Ise-Shima. For Peter Watson*)

I

Here, where the Pacific seems a pond,
Winds like pocket knives have carved out islands
From sandstone, to *netsuke*:
                              Pekingese,
With rampant ruffs and fan-spread claws,
Scratch at coiff'd waves.
                              A pirate junk
Lobs cones from conifers (its mast
That solitary pine trunk staved
With two dead boughs).
                              Porcupine,
Tortoise, dragon, cormorant.

II

                              Our boat throbs on
Through sea and sky, the seamless bowl
Of solid light in which pearl fishers dive.
It thrusts through scarcely lifting waves;
– Long rollers moving under silk –
A stretching and unstretching surface.
Fisherboats are delicate
As water-boatmen.

III

                              We land
Where a path skirts the rocks. Twined ropes
Are slung between two boulders to lasso
At dawn the sun, risen for pilgrims.
Following the path, I reach a park

With cliffs hewn into caves embossed
With hieroglyphs . . .

                    In one cave,
A hermit sits. He scrapes a tune
Upon one hair outstretched of his white beard.
His bow's his bone-thin arm.

   IV

Suddenly I hear your voice,
Inside my skull, peal – like the tongue
Inside a pilgrim's bell – peal out
In those gay mocking tones I knew:

                              'You were
Once my companion on a journey
The far side of the world, the Alps,
Rock-leaded windows of Europe.
You saw fields diamonded as harlequin
Reflected on my laughing eyes, who now
Am dragged under the soil in a net
That tangles smile and eyeballs with
Their visions rainbowed still.

                    But you,
Lacking my eyes through which you looked,
Turn like a shadow round the sunlit dial.'

Fifteen-line Sonnet in Four Parts

   I

When we talk, I imagine silence
Beyond the intervalling words: a space
Empty of all but ourselves there, face to face,
Away from others, alone in the intense
Light or dark, it would not matter which.

303

II

But where a room envelops us, one heart,
Our bodies, locked together, prove apart
Unless we change them back again to speech.

III

Close to you here, looking at you, I see
Beyond your eyes looking back, that second you
Of whom the outward semblance is the image –
The inward being where the name springs true.

IV

Today, left only with a name, I rage,
Willing these lines – willing a name to be
Flesh, on the blank unanswering page.

What Love Poems Say

In spite of this
Enormity of space –
Total distance total dark between
Lights all ice all fire
Adverse to all of life –

Nevertheless, I wake
This morning to this luck, that you
On a second of a clock
Into a measured space, this room,
Come, as though
Spiralling down a staircase of
Immeasurable light-years –
Here and Now made flesh,
With greeting in your eyes,

Lips smiling, willing to respond,
Hand extended.

It is as though I were
In all the universe the centre
Of a circumference
Surrounding us with lights
That have eyes watchful, benevolent –
Looked on us and concentrated
Their omnipresence in one instance –
You, come with a word.

Four Sketches for Herbert Read

INNOCENCE

Farm house, green field. Stone
White in grey eyes.
The innocent gaze
Simplifies forms
To rectangle, circle.
The sun in the skull
Dissolves a world to light.

YOUNG OFFICER

Young officer, leaning
Against a bayonet hedge
Of blackthorn, its white
Blossom, your medals.
Your soldiers graze
Like sheep. You are their shepherd.
Mournful bugles
Engraved those lines
Either side your mouth.

I took a pencil up
Idly at some conference,
Drew the lick of hair
Surround to your face.
The bow tie beneath
Marked a question mark's dot.
In the hall of chairs
Fat platitudes sat.
You stood out like a question.

When you died, I was in France.
Supposing you were sad –
Listen. I saw the students
Thread the streets in dance.
Their heels struck fire.
Their hands uprooted pavements.
Their mouths sang the chant
Of a poet's final hour:
Imagination seizes power.

To W. H. Auden on His Sixtieth Birthday

You – the young bow-tied near-albino undergraduate
With rooms on Peck Quad (blinds drawn down at midday
To shut the sun out) – read your poems aloud
In so clinical a voice, I thought
You held each word gleaming on forceps
Up to your lamp. Images seemed segments
On slides under the iciest of microscopes
Which showed white edges round dark stains
Of the West collapsing to a farce:
Not to be wept over, since the ruins

Offered the poet a bare-kneed engineer's
Chance of scrambling madly over scrap heaps
To fish out carburettors, sparking plugs,
A sculptured Hell from a cathedral porch,
Scenes from sagas and a water-logged
Lost code. With nicotine-stained fingers
You rigged such junk into new, strange machines.
Two met at dawn (riders against the sky line),
A spy crouched on the floor of a parched cistern,
One with hands that clutched at the wet reeds
Was shot, escaping. Your words lobbed squibs
Into my solemn dream, the young Romantic's
Praying his wound would blossom to a rose
Of blood, vermilion under a gold moon,
Exclaiming – 'O!'
                          Forty years later, now, benevolent
In carpet slippers, you still make devices,
Sitting at table, playing patience,
Grumpily fitting our lives to your game
Whose rules are dogma of objective love.

One More New Botched Beginning

Their voices heard, I stumble suddenly
Choking in undergrowth. I'm torn
Mouth pressed against the thorns,
                                        remembering
Ten years ago, here in Geneva
I walked with Merleau-Ponty by the lake.
Upon his face, I saw his intellect.
Energy of the sun-interweaving
Waves, electric, danced on him. His eyes
Smiled with their gay logic through
Black coins flung down from leaves.
                                        He who

Was Merleau-Ponty that day is no more
Irrevocable than the I that day who was
Beside him – I'm still living!

   Also that summer
My son stayed up the valley in the mountains.
One day I went to see him and he stood
Not seeing me, watching some hens.
Doing so, he was absorbed
In their wire-netted world. He danced
On one leg. Leaning forward, he became
A bird-boy. I am there
Still seeing him. To him
That moment – unselfknowing even then
Is drowned in the oblivious earliness . . .

                          Such pasts
Are not diminished distances, perspective
Vanishing points, but doors
Burst open suddenly by gusts
That seek to blow the heart out . . .
                          Today I see
Three undergraduates standing talking in
A college quad. They show each other poems –
Louis MacNeice, Bernard Spencer, and I.
Louis caught cold in the rain, Bernard fell
From a train door.

Their lives are now those poems that were
Pointers to the poems to be their lives.
We read there in the college quad. Each poem
Is still a new beginning. If
They had been finished though they would have died
Before they died. Being alive
Is when each moment's a new start, with past
And future shuffled between fingers
For a new game.

                                        I'm dealing out
My hand to them, one more new botched beginning,
Here, where we still stand talking in the quad.

Matter of Identity

Who he was, remained an open question
He asked himself, looking at all those others –
The Strangers, roaring down the street.

Explorer, politician, bemedalled
General, teacher – any of these
He might have been. But he was none.

Impossible though, to avoid the conclusion
That he had certain attributes: for instance,
Parents, birthdays, sex. Calendars

Each year the same day totted up his age.
Also, he was a husband and had children
And fitted in his office, measure to his desk.

Yet he never felt quite certain
Even of certainties: discerned a gap
(Like that between two letters) between statistics

(These he was always writing out on forms)
And his real self. Sometimes he wondered
Whether he had ever been born, or had died . . .

(A blank space dreaming of its asterisks)

        *   *   *

Sometimes he had the sensation
Of being in a library, and reading a history

And coming to a chapter left unwritten
That blazed with nothing . . . nothing except him
. . . Nothing but his great name and his great deeds.

To Become a Dumb Thing

Sunset.
At the harbour mouth headlands of agate.
Lamps stab needles into the pleating water.
Fishermen stand or sit, at quayside, in boats, mending nets.
One, without a word, gets up, goes over to another, helps him,
   goes back.

   *

We sit at our café table by the waves.
Talk Paris New York London places we shall/shan't visit.
The temples! The bullring! The blood!
Red hot corpses shed into the Ganges!
Gossip! Friends! Enemies!
Playing over worn scenes on a worn reel.

   *

Six fishermen wade out. Clamber onto a boat. One advances
to the end of the jetty to which several boats, with men and
women on them, are tied. He pisses into the sea.

   *

Their life is things. Their thoughts are things.
They touch things. The fish nudges against the hook. The
hook pricks the gullet. The line tugs against the horn
hand. The nets balance moon-glittering scales.

   *

At day's end the sun, a raging ball, topples them over
one by one. Falling into beds. Flailing arms. Into
one another. Drunk.

   *

To be them would mean throwing aside Christian's burden
when he forsook wife and children . . .
to . . .

unwind this coil . . .
crawling on all fours . . .
begging life from beggars . . .
to become a dumb thing.

Bagatelles

I AFTER THE INSCRIPTION ON A GREEK STELE OF A WOMAN
HOLDING HER GRANDCHILD ON HER KNEES

My daughter's dear child here I hold on my lap: so
I used to hold him of old in those days
When with living eyes we both looked on the sun:
Now that he's dead, I still hold him: for I
Am dead too.

II M.J. (1940)

That running boy with mouth raised up
Hands stretched towards the winning cup
Eyes starting forth: lies on the ground
His victory drained away through a small wound.

III FOR HUMPHRY HOUSE

When you became a Christian, mocking (not mocking) I said
'Then bless me!' You growled 'Kneel!' So I knelt down there in
    the High.
I carry this like an amulet always. You know –
If you watch from bright air under earth where you lie.

IV SENTENCED

He thought of the blank paper as
Where he should be what he was:
His writing, as the sap that flows
Along the stem into the rose.

Words, straight from the heart, his song
Being from his heart, could not go wrong.
All he had to do was be
His real self blazing through the tree.
So he wrote, without pretence
His truth.
        That was his youth.
                Each sentence
Stands written in his book.
                Indeed,
His sentence there for all to read.

V DESCARTES

Lightning, enlightening, turns
Midnight to one flash of white.
Startled, people, steeples, hens
Shudder into sight.
Dogs bark. Cocks crow. Descartes
Writes in chalk across black sky:
I think therefore I
Am. Words a sponge deletes.
Black blackness blackens.

VI MOSQUITO

Filigree mosquito
Afloat in black air
Anchors above my head,
Tinsel trumpet blowing
In the tomb of my ear.
Angel of Fra Angelico
Awakening me, dead,
To such thoughts as make
Midnight Judgement Day.

VII MOON

Moon, I don't believe in you!
Yet now I almost do
Seeing you (above those rectangles
Of windows – triangles
Of roofs – squares of squares –
And through those scimitars
Of silhouetted leaves)
Describe your lucid circle –
Exultant disk buoying up
A map that mocks our Earth.

VIII PRESENT ABSENCE

You slept so quiet at your end of the room, you seemed
A memory, your absence.
I worked well, rising early, while you dreamed.
I thought your going would only make this difference:
A memory, your presence.
But now I am alone I know a silence
That howls. Here solitude begins.

IX AFTER TIBULLUS

Absolute passion which I thought I'd shown
These past few days to thee, my sole delight,
Let me no more make boast of, if I've done
Ever one act that caused me greater shame,
Bitterer self-reproach, than that last night:
The offence of leaving thee all night alone,
Through seeking to dissimulate my flame.

X A POLITICAL GENERATION

When they put pen
To paper, in those times,
They knew their written

Ten lines with five rhymes,
Before the reader had turned
The page over, might have burned.

With such doubts, how could they doubt
Their duty – to write
Poems that put fires out
To keep lights alight?
So, putting first things first,
They did their best to write their worst.

XI TO MY JAPANESE TRANSLATOR (SHOZO)

My English writing runs into your eyes
Then reappears along your finger tips
And through the brush upon the paper
In characters – to me – snow crystals.

We look into each other's faces:
In mine, your eyes, in yours, mine, opposite.
Midway between us both, our tongues
Change you to me and me to you.

XII RENAISSANCE HERO

A galaxy of cells composed a system
Where he was, human, in his tower of bones.
The sun rose in his head. The moon ran, full,
Vermilion in the blood along his veins.
His statue stood in marble in his glance.

Body and intellect in him were one.
Raised but his hand, and through the universe
Relations altered between things in space.
Before his step, light opened like a door.
Time took the seal of his intaglio face.

Central Heating System

I'm woken up
By the central heating system. An engine
Thuds in the cellar. Steam clanks in pipes
With distinct sounds – cymbals banged together.
The snow falls outside
Hushing up the scandal of the dark,
Whitewashing the blackness of the boughs.
But here, in the room, the pipes must make their scene.
Like a long watch dog curled through the whole house,
They bark at the ice-fanged killer
Who leaves no footstep in the night.

(*Storrs, Connecticut*)

Art Student

With ginger hair dragged over
                        fiery orange face
Blue shirt, red scarf knotted round his neck,
Blue jeans, soft leather Russian boots
Tied round with bands he ties and unties when
His feet are not spread sprawling on two tables –
Yawning, he reads his effort. It's about
A crazy Icarus always falling into
A labyrinth.
           He says
He only has one subject – death – he don't know why –
And saying so leans back scratching his head
Like a Dickensian coachman.
                    Apologizes
For his bad verse – he's no poet – an art student –
– Paints – sculpts – has to complete a work at once
Or loses faith in it.
               Anyway, he thinks

Art's finished.
                    There's only one thing left
Go to the slaughter house and fetch
A bleeding something-or-other – oxtail, heart,
Bollocks, or best a bullock's pair of lungs,
Then put them in the college exhibition,
On a table or hung up on a wall
Or if they won't allow that, just outside
In the courtyard.
                    (Someone suggests
He put them in a plastic bag. He sneers at that.)

The point is they'll produce some slight sensation –
Shock, indignation, admiration. He bets
Some student will stand looking at them
For hours on end and find them beautiful
Just as he finds any light outside a gallery,
On a junk heap of automobiles, for instance,
More beautiful than sunsets framed inside.
That's all we can do now – send people back
To the real thing – the stinking corpse.

1974–1985

Cyril Connolly, November 1974

This hews you to your statue:
Flakes away the flesh
Back to bone intellect;
Lays bare the brow, pure semi-circle.
Star-striking dome –
Sidera sublime vertice –
Proves finally your head was Roman.

This seals your eyelids; sharpens
The nose, so sensual once,
To a pure triangle; this drills
Into the base, the nostrils.

     Hid in the creviced mouth
Only the palate still
Savours the must of dying.

     She who leans over
Your shoulder, from which the sheet
Stretches in outline to the feet,
Tugs it to make you
Recognize me: 'Don't! I pray, don't!
Don't let him see me seeing
His onyx eyeballs shout at me from marble!'

[1975]

From My Diary

'She was,' my father said (in an aside)
'A great beauty, forty years ago.'
Out of my crude childhood, I stared at
Our tottering hostess, trembling
In her armchair, pouring tea from silver –

Her pink silk dress, her pale blue gaze –
I only saw her being sixty-five,
I could not see the girl my father saw.

Now that I'm older than my father then was
I go with lifelong friends to the same parties
Which we have gone to always
We seem the same age always
Although the parties sometimes change to funerals
That sometimes used to change to christenings.

Faces we've once loved
Fit into their Seven Ages of Man as Russian dolls
Fit into one another. My X-Ray memory
Penetrates through the several covers
Of the successive dolls back to the face
That I first saw. So when the exterior final
Doll is laid under its final lid
Your glowing firstseen face shines through them all.

[1975]

A Souvenir of Cincy

*A postcard for John Betjeman, once Elliston Professor at the
University of Cincinnati, a position which the writer had occupied
two years previously.*

Remember how
  A quarter of a century ago, in Cincinnati,
  After monochrome winter, at last May
  Painted blossoms in a light blue sky
  Japanese double cherry, peach, plum – petals –
  In their green chalices. Then suddenly
  One night a blizzard swooped
  From the white Arctic down the plains through blackness
  Whirling knives of ice and scarves of snow. Yet when

We woke next morning, that dervish had roared past.
The innocuous sun
Unperturbed re-entered
The domed sky curved around it, bent a deeper
Wept-out blue. And each blossom
Japanese double cherry, peach, plum – petals –
Was separately encased in ice.
They glittered in their millions in the sun.
Within an hour the ice had melted. Petals dropped
Like moulted pigeon feathers on slush side walks,
Trampled on by galoshes
Of people hurrying to their work.

[1982]

Adam

After García Lorca

Morning by tree of blood is moistened
Where the newly delivered woman groans.
Her voice leaves crystals in the wound
And in the window a print of bones.

While the light comes in secure and gains
White boundaries of oblivious fable
In the race from the turmoil of the veins
Into the clouded coolness of the apple,

Adam dreams in the fever of clay
Of a child who draws near galloping
With the double throb of his cheek its way.

But another darker Adam sleeping
Dreams of neuter seedless stone moon afar
Where the child of light is kindling.

[1985]

Louis MacNeice

Like skyscrapers with high windows staring down from the
    sun,
Some faces suggest
Elevation. Their way-up eyes
Look down at you diagonally and their aloof
Hooded glance suggests
A laugh turning somersaults in some high penthouse
Of their skulls. Seeing such a one
Looking down at you, smiling to himself, you can't help
Looking down at yourself from his point of view: at the top of
Your bald head, for instance
Where the one brushed-back copper-dyed hair is noted
With precise irony. Louis
MacNeice was
Like that. Leaning
Against a marble chimney piece
With one elbow an angle in a Picasso cubist portrait,
The superior head slanted back
With dancing eyes summing you up
And laughter only just arrested
At some joke about you, known only to himself
(Perhaps the cutting phrase sharpening in his forehead)
He half-beckoned you up into his high mind
For a shared view of your clumsiness –
I mean, me, of mine.

Now, reading his poem 'Bagpipe Music', I don't know how to
    pronounce
C-e-i-l-i-d-h – nor what it means –
He looks down from high heaven
The mocking eyes search-lighting
My ignorance again.

   [1985]

322

A Girl Who Has Drowned Herself Speaks

If only they hadn't shown that cruel mercy
Of dredging my drowned body from the river
That locked me in its peace, up to their surface
Of autopsy, and burial and forms –
This, which was my last wish, might have come true –
That when the waves had finally washed away
The remnants of my flesh, the skull would stay –
But change to crystal. Things outside
Which it had looked at once, would swim into
Eye sockets that looked at them: through
The scooped-out caverns of the skull, would dart
Solid phosphorescent fish, where there had been
Their simulacra only in the brain.

[1985]

Late Stravinsky Listening to Late Beethoven

'At the end, he listened only to
Beethoven's last quartets.
Some we played so often
You could only hear the needle in the groove.'

She smiled,
Lightly touching her cheek.

I see you on your bed under the ceiling
Weightless as your spirit, happiness
Shining through pain. You have become
Purged of every self but the transparent
Intelligence, through which the sounds revolve
Their furious machine. With delectation
You watch Beethoven rage, hammer
Crash plucked strings, escape

On wings transfiguring horizons: transcend
The discords in his head that were
The prisoning bars of deafness.

                                    He only knew
That there was music which went on outside
That in his mind, through seeing sound: for example,
Walking through the Wiener Wald
One loud spring day, he saw a shepherd
Playing his flute against the hillside,
And knew there was the tune because he saw it
Delineated by the flute.
Then stumping down the fields into the valley,
Saw cymbals clash beneath steep banks
Where, on the river, blocks of ice
Collided: saw too, high up,
The wind pluck strings of willow harps
Against the brass of sky.
                              His eyes became
Windows in the skull through which he looked
Out on a world of sound.
                              Above
A base of mountain peaks, a bird, a violin,
Sustains a curve, a tune, parabola,
Held in the eye become an ear: flies on
Until the line at last dissolves
Into that light where the perceiver
Becomes one with the thing perceived,
The hearing with the seeing,
                              Beethoven
Released from deafness into vision,
Stravinsky in that music from his dying.

  [1985]

Auden's Funeral

One among friends who stood above your grave
I cast a clod of earth from those heaped there
Down on the great brass-handled coffin lid.
It rattled on the oak like a door knocker
And at that sound I saw your face beneath
Wedged in an oblong shadow under ground.
Flesh creased, eyes shut, jaw jutting
And on the mouth a grin: triumph of one
Who has escaped from life-long colleagues roaring
For him to join their throng. He's still half with us
Conniving slyly, yet he knows he's gone
Into that cellar where they'll never find him,
Happy to be alone, his last work done,
Word freed from world, into a different wood.

II

But we, with feet on grass, feeling the wind
Whip blood up in our cheeks, walk back along
The hillside road we earlier climbed today
Following the hearse and tinkling village band.
The white October sun circles Kirchstetten
With colours of chrysanthemums in gardens,
And bronze and golden under wiry boughs,
A few last apples gleam like jewels.
Back in the village inn, we sit on benches
For the last toast to you, the honoured ghost
Whose absence now becomes incarnate in us.
Tasting the meats, we imitate your voice
Speaking in flat benign objective tones
The night before you died. In the packed hall
You are your words. Your listeners see

Written on your face the poems they hear
Like letters carved in a tree's bark
The sight and sound of solitudes endured.
And looking down on them, you see
Your image echoed in their eyes
Enchanted by your language to be theirs.
And then, your last word said, halloing hands
Hold up above their heads your farewell bow.
Then many stomp the platform, entreating
Each for his horde, your still warm signing hand.
But you have hidden away in your hotel
And locked the door and lain down on the bed
And fallen from their praise, dead on the floor.

III

(Ghost of a ghost, of you when young, you waken
In me my ghost when young, us both at Oxford.
You, the tow-haired undergraduate
With jaunty liftings of the head.
Angular forward stride, cross-questioning glance,
A Buster Keaton-faced pale *gravitas*.
Saying aloud your poems whose letters bit
Ink-deep into my fingers when I set
Them up upon my five-pound printing press:

'*An evening like a coloured photograph*

A music stultified across the water

The heel upon the finishing blade of grass.')

IV

Back to your room still growing memories –
Handwriting, bottles half-drunk, and us – drunk –
Chester, in prayers, still prayed for your 'dear C.',
Hunched as Rigoletto, spluttering

Ecstatic sobs, already slanted
Down towards you, his ten-months-hence
Grave in Athens – remembers
Opera, your camped-on heaven, odourless
Resurrection of your bodies singing
Passionate duets whose chords resolve
Your rows in harmonies. Remembers
Some tragi-jesting wish of yours and puts
'Siegfried's Funeral March' on the machine.
Wagner who drives out every thought but tears –
Down-crashing drums and cymbals cataclysmic
End-of-world brass exalt on drunken waves
The poet's corpse borne on a bier beyond
The foundering finalities, his world,
To that Valhalla where the imaginings
Of the dead makers are their lives.
The dreamer sleeps forever with the dreamed.

 v

Then night. Outside your porch we linger
Murmuring farewells, thinking tomorrows
Separate like those stars above.
Gone from our feast, your life enters your poems
Like music heard transformed into notes seen.
Your funeral dwindles to its photograph
In black and white, of friends around your grave.
This dark obliterates all. Farewell,
The magic instrument of consciousness
With intellect like rays exposing
Lives driven out on the circumference
Of this time, their explosion: O, but making
Paradigms of love, the poems
That draw them back into the circle,
Of your enfolding solitude.

 [1985]

Choruses from THE OEDIPUS TRILOGY (1985)

from Oedipus Rex

I

O thrilling voice of Zeus
        come from Apollo's golden shrine
        with what intent towards us

            I tremble I faint I fail
            terror racks my soul

O Delian healer to whom my cries
from this abyss of despair arise

        What fate unknown until now
        or lost in the past and renewed
drawn from the revolving years
        will you send to us

O speak o tell me, immortal voice

        To Athena, daughter of Zeus,
     and her sister, Artemis,
        and Apollo of fiery arrows
     triple guardians of Thebes
          I call

If ever before in time past
you saved us from plague or defeat
        turn back to us now, and save!

  The plague invades
  No knowledge saves
  birth pangs of women
  bring forth dead their children
  life on life sped
  to the land of the dead

like birds wing on wing
struck down from their flying
to the parched earth
by the marksman death

O Delian healer hear my prayer
star of my hope in my night of despair

grant that this god who without clash of sword on shield
fills with cries of our dying Thebes he makes his battlefield
turn back in flight from us
be made to yield

driven by great gales favouring our side

to the far Thracian waters wave on wave
where none found haven ever but his grave

O Zeus come with thy lightning to us save

And come back Bacchus
hair gold-bound and cheeks flame-red
whom the Bacchantae worship and the Maenads led
by his bright torch on high

Revelling again among us Bacchus and make death
The god whom gods and men most hate lie dead.

II

If I still have the gift of prophecy,
O hills and valleys of lovely Cythaeron,
I swear that by tomorrow at full moon
Oedipus will recognize in you
Mother and nurse and native land he grew in.
So these, because they pleased our king, we sing
And to Apollo may they too prove pleasing.

Who was it fathered you, and who conceived you,
Child, among these hills, by moon or noon?
Was it to Pan some wandering nymph bore you

While he roamed the mountainside? Or may it have been
Some bride Apollo favoured? Or even
Bacchus, god of the Bacchantae, received you,
A gift from a nymph on Helicon,
One of those he most delights to play with?

III

O human generations, I consider
Life but a shadow. Where is the man
Ever attained more than the semblance
Of happiness but it quickly vanished?
Oedipus, I count your life the example
Proving we can call no human blessed.

With skill incomparable he threw the spear;
He gained the prize of an unchallenged fame;
He killed the crooked-taloned maiden
Whose singing made the midday darken;
He was our tower that rose up against death
And from that day we called him King of Thebes.

But now whose history is more grievous
Plagued with the loss of all that greatness his?
Whose fortune ever met with such reverse?
I pity Oedipus for whom that soft flesh couch
That bore him, also proved his nuptial couch,
Oh how can soil in which your father sowed
Have secretly endured your seed so long?

Time, all-revealing, finally tracked you down,
Condemned the monstrous marriage which begot
Your children upon her, your own begetter.
O son of Laius, would my eyes had never seen you.
I weep like one with lips formed for lament.
Until today it was you who gave me light;
Today your darkness covers up my eyes.

from Oedipus at Colonos

I

Stranger, this is shining Colonos,
Famed for horses, loveliest place.
Nightingales pour forth their song
From wine-dark depths of ivy where they dwell
Close to the god's inviolable bowers,
Heavy with fruit and never visited
By scorching sun or rending wind.
Here Dionysus revelling runs
The nymphs that nursed him, his companions.

Each dawn narcissus clusters, washed
In the sky dew, upraise their crowns,
Those worn of old by the great goddesses,
And crocuses like shafts of sunlight show.
Fed by eternal streams, the fountains
Of Cephysus fan through the plains
Bringing their swelling breasts increase.
Nor are the Muses absent from this place.

And here a miracle, a thing unknown
In Asia, flourishes perpetually –
The self-renewing vast-trunked olive tree,
A bastion for us against enemies
And, for Athenian children, nurturer.
Nor youth nor age can cause it damage
For Zeus smiles on it, and grey-eyed
Athena holds it in her keeping gaze.

But most of all, I have to praise the horse,
Poseidon's gift to this land, glorious,
Running beside white horses of the waves.
And Colonos is where Poseidon taught
Man bit and bridle for the horse the horse

To tame the wild colt and to curb his speed:
And taught him carve the wood for prows and oars
Chasing the Nereids through the waves.

II

Whoever craves a longer life than his allotted span
That man
I count a fool. For what do more days add
But to his sum of grief, and not of pleasure,
If he endure beyond the appointed measure?

The curtain falls the same, in any case.
When his superfluous days are done;
Youth, wedding, dance, song, death itself
Are one.

Best, never to have been born at all; the next best is
Quick turn back to nothing whence he came.

For after tasting youth's soon-passed
Feather-head follies, then what troubles
Do not crowd in on him:
Faction, envy, murder, wars, and last
Senility claims its own:
Unsociable,
Infirm, unfriended, shunned by all.

Oedipus is old: a promontory
Exposed on every side to storms
The elemental forces overwhelm,
Every disaster falling on him: come
From sunrise and the sunset, from
The icy north, torrid meridian,
All day – and all night long, the glittering stars.

from Antigone

Happy are those who never tasted evil.
For once the house incurs the rage of heaven
The indignant curse fallen on it never ceases
But remains always, and for ever passes
From life to life through all its generations.

So from the earliest times the sorrows
Of children of the house of Labdacus
Heap on their dead new sorrows always
Never set free by later generations,
And if a son arise to free that house
A god arises soon to cast him down.

Just as when howling gales from off-shore
Pile up in mountainous waves the Thracian seas
Fathoms above the shadowy sea floor,
These suck up from the depths black sands
Which, risen, spread over all the surface
While the storm roars against the headlands.

Now, of the house of Oedipus, that hope
Which was the last extension of the root,
That light which promised so much is put out,
By bloodstained dust that was a debt
Unpaid to the infernal gods,
And by a young girl's frenzied heart.

DOLPHINS (1994)

Dolphins

Happy, they leap
Out of the surface
Of waves reflecting
The sun fragmented
To broken glass
By the stiff breeze
Across our bows.

Curving, they draw
Curlicues
And serifs with
Lashed tail and fin
Across the screen
Of blue horizon –
Images
Of their delight
Outside, displaying
My heart within.

Across this dazzling
Mediterranean
August morning
The dolphins write such
Ideograms:
With power to wake
Me prisoned in
My human speech
They sign:
'I AM!'

Her House

The city left behind them, they drove on
Past factories, suburbs, farms.

                              She saw
Suddenly, from a hill, the coast
Outlined by surf, and rocks that seemed
The shadows of the surf.
                              'My house!' she cried,
Pointing in triumph where it stood
High on a cliff above a bay.

The slate roof gleamed like dove feathers
And in the fanned façade tall windows
Mirrored on glass panes the garden
Between whose dazzling colours loomed
The shadowy interior
Cut through with glints of gold.

'My house!
My house for which I've scraped and saved
These thirty years! My house I've driven
All day to boast to you, dear friend!'

    Leaving the main road then, she drove
Down a steep lane between tall hedges
Whose branches, high up, interlocked.
'This tunnel of dense leaves,' she thought,
'Is minutes of eternity
Through which I have to press to reach my house.'

But when at last she reached the light,
All she was sure was hers had vanished
– No house, no friend, no car.
                              She was
Alone, dressed in a shroud, beholding
The quivering fury of the desert
Where crackling thorn and cactus blazed.

    *

        High on a sandstone cliff, there stood
Figures in shrouds hewn out of sandstone

Who raised grave hands in salutation
To her who, kneeling to them, prayed:
'Have you no nook or cranny to let me in?'

And woke elate in certainty
She shared the eternal desert, theirs.

Lines for Roy Fuller

Lines of yours I first read were of war
In Africa: your being *moved across*
Two oceans and *bored systematically*
By army life: and your eyes opened onto
Ultimate truth: which is – *the terrible*.

Reading your words then, I saw soldiers
Silhouetted against bare sky
With their machines: those instruments
For killing, being killed: tank, gun,
In the arena of the scorpion.

One flesh-like thing was that mauve flower
Which, between thorns, the cactus shows:
Defenceless as those young men's faces
Naked above their battle dress –
Their camouflage of scrub and sand.

Carpaccio painted such a scene:
Soldiers – helmets – breast-plates – skulls –
Cactus – a dragon. Standing there,
A hermit with eyes deep as wells
Piercing the desert, like your lines.

Air Raid

In this room like a bowl of flowers filled with light
Family eyes look down on the white
Pages of a book, and the white ceiling
Like starch of a nurse, reflects a calm feeling.

The daughter, with hands outstretched to the fire,
Transmits through her veins the peaceful desire
Of the family tree, from which she was born,
To push tendrils through dark to a happier dawn.

In the ancient house or the glass-and-steel flat
The vertical descendants of the genes that
Go back far in the past, are supported by floors
And protected by walls from the weather outdoors.

In their complex stage settings they act out the parts
Of their bodies enclosing their human hearts
With limbs utilizing chairs, tables, cups,
All the necessities and props.

They wear the right clothes and go the right ways,
Read the news, and play golf, and fill out their days
With hobbies, meals brought from the kitchen range.
And no one sees anything eerie or strange

In all this. And perhaps they are right. Nothing is
Until an unreasoning fury impinges
From an enemy's vision of life, on their hearth.
And explodes. And tears their loved home down to earth.

Then the inside-turned-outside faces the street.
Rubble decently buries the dead human meat.
Piled above it, a bath, wardrobe, books, telephone
Though all who could answer its ringing have gone.

Standing unscathed is one solitary wall,
Half a floor attached, forgotten to fall.

Convolvulus patterns of pink and blue line
That rectangle high up where they once used to dine.

Bemused passers-by are bound to observe
That inside-shown-outside like the deep curve
Of mother-o'-pearl exposed in a shell
Where a mollusc, long smashed, at one time did dwell.

But the house has been cracked in an enemy's claws,
Years of love ground down to rubble in jaws,
And the tender sensitive life thrown away
By the high-flying will of the enemy's day.

  [*Horizon*, February 1941. 1993]

Letter from an Ornithologist in Antarctica

  (*Remembering S.B.O.*)

Happy, you write, I am, happy to go alone
On the cable chair from Palmer Station (where our base is)
Across 'Hero Inlet' to 'Bonaparte Point'
(Just a bare rock attached to a crumbling glacier!)
Where at night I fumble stones for baby petrels
Until the cold has made my fingers freeze –
And I cannot tell the chicks apart from stones
Nor feel the cable well for my return.

Most nights are cloudy, always overcast,
But sometimes I peek stars through cloud-rifts –
Once Halley's Comet in a cloud ripped open.

One night the sky was clear, no wind, air balmy,
And I lay snug in gloves and sweater
Happy to be alone but also happy
To think of my companions nearby
Connected to me by that cable –
And that six hundred miles far north the tip

Of Tierra del Fuego has some settlers
(Four hundred further north there come real towns).

Then, as I watched the sky, I saw six stars
Move, and I speculated that space satellites
– Those man-made messengers on starry errands
Of espionage, war, TV – good or evil –
Converge over the Pole. Happy I felt then
Out there, in space, those distances made human.

Farewell to My Student

For our farewell, we went down to the footpath
Circling the lake.
                    You stood there, looking up at
Egrets nesting in high branches

– White ghosts in a green tapestry.

    And I stood silent, thinking of
Images to recall this moment.

The first must surely be that pine tree
Bark slashed with gold, leaning across
The blue lines of the lake beyond.

    Then, stamped upon the day, your face.

                    Perhaps Bellini
Delved from antiquity such an image
Of a twenty-year-old Triton, against waves
Blowing on a conch;

And Seurat, centuries later, in the profile
Of a hallooing boy against the Seine.

    But then you turned to me and said
With that mild glance, a third thing to remember:

'You are gone already, your thoughts far from here
At least three thousand miles away
Where you will be tomorrow.'

Then ten years passed till, today, I write these lines.

Laughter

That time you laughed
Fell over on the floor laughing

And then my laughter too caught fire
One blaze of both our laughing

Remembered across distances long after

Not gone not gone not altogether
Extinguished by the Ice Age of your death.

When you were living
It lingered in the world
Among things only put aside
In cupboards – letters, clothes,
Photographs taken on that journey
We went together

All now become
On one side – yours – pure absence
On mine, that vacuum
Nature, we are told, abhors:

Which now the memory of our laughing
Rushes in to fill.

History and Reality

'Sin is nothing but the refusal to recognize human misery.'
Simone Weil

I

Escaped from Germany –
Cared for by English friends, with whom
Kindness counted still –

Rumours reached her –

Photographs made by the Gestapo –

Jews, her people –
So various, all one –

Each taken full-face –

The strong – the meek – the sad – the proud

*

Hunger had stretched the parchment skin
Across the contours of the bone –
Forehead, cheek-bones, chin.

And in each face there was the same
Ultimate revelation
Of eyes that stared upon the real –

Some terrible final thing.

II

She locked herself inside her room,
Her mind filled with those images
From Germany, her homeland, where
Those deaths were the reality –

Real! – not some tragedy that actors
Performed before an audience –

Pity and terror purifying
The onlooker, enraptured by
Poetry secreted in the lines.
But where the players were the victims
Massacred from a tyrant's mouth.

*

She felt a kind of envy for
Those who stood naked in their truth:
Where to be of her people was
To be one of those millions killed.

III

She starved her body to pure thought
To be one with her people snatched
From ghettos by the SS, then
Hurled into cattle trucks of trains
Hurtling all night across bare plains
Till dawn, when there stood, waiting on
Platforms of sidings (below walls
Of concrete and barbed wire) – guards, who
Marched them to a parade-ground, where
Those fit to work in factories
Were separated from the rest –
Women and children, the old, the sick,
Who, taken to a yard, were robbed
Of jewellery, satchels, playthings, shoes –
Things that to them meant home and name –
And made to stand there when a voice
From a watch-tower proclaimed they would
Be cleansed of lice, and being Jews.

IV

Then thrust inside a shed where she
Through her intense imagining
Stood there among them bodily

When, from outside, the guards turned on
Taps through which hissed not water but
The murdering gas, whereon that crowd
Breathed a great sigh of revelation –
Their life, their death – for her the real
Instant where history ground its wheel
On her with them, inside that moment
When – outside – truth was only words.

The Half of Life

(*To Barry Humphries*)

Half his life gone, he takes his drink
In the café in the park. Across
Oblongs of marble table-tops
Lights and shadows travel, arrowing from
The sun, through wind-stirred leaves above.

Lifting his spoon, he lets it ring
Idly against his glass, and thinks
'The time that took to sound sums up
All my life lived till now, contained
Within the instant it was struck.

'But when I leave here, setting out
On that half life that's still to come,
Each lived-through moment will weigh on
My pulses – work, war, boredom, love –
Experienced each as a whole world.

'Then, at the end, when I return
To sit down here at my old place
Amongst those young as I am now
(I'll think "They're young as I was then")
All my past life will seem one shadow
Cast by the sun on a white stone.'

The Palatine Anthology

(To Charles Causley)

Above, there is a firmament of stars
Two thousand light-years distant from us.

Some names still pierce us with their light
Anacreon, Callimachus –

Plato still scrawls across those skies:
'Would that I had your million eyes
To gaze down on my friend – star-gazing
From Earth. His eyes would have no choice
Then, but meet mine.'

One poet is *Anonymous*:

Out of his whole life he chose
This instant of intensest flame!
Having attained which climax, he
Let fall a canister through space –

His burned-out no-name.

Have-beens

                     have sometimes the feeling
That they're not here at all, not of this day
Ordered by the clock-hand in every particular
All over the world, the ticking minute,
But of another place that has no time-table
Except in having been all equally buried
Under the lid, the crust of the present,
In Hades where all pasts are contemporaneous
Simply in having been: the swords shields helmets
Of the *Iliad*'s prehistory, in the same junkyard
As the shells and dug-outs of the Western Front.

Poètes Maudits

I BRUSSELS 1873

Under the X-ray sun, two *poètes*
Maudits sit drinking absinthe: *Paul*,
Lecherously lachrymose at having
Abandoned wife, child, priest, for *Rimb*,
Heaven-born boy with Hellfire tongue,
Hair a torn halo round his head
And eyes that gaze deep in his glass.

Drunken on language, they hurl down,
In rivalry between them, boasts –
Each clamouring he had the more
Obscene childhood, spent all day
Crouching in holes of latrines, spying
Up at those parts the grown-ups hide
Under pious hypocrisies
Of hymns sung, sermons preached, in church:
Cocks cunts arse-holes from out of whose
Passages issue piss shit blood,
Excremental extremities
Dictionaries grudge four letters to
And doctors bury in deep tomes
Of dead words in dead languages
Like Latin names inscribed on tombs.

Delirious with ecstasy
Of shames let fly against the sun
Rimb leaps up on the table, tears
His clothes apart above the knees
And shows embossed upon one thigh
A cicatrice like a medallion.
'My gilded stamp of sin,' he cries,
'That I was born with, my true self.'

Ecstatic at such innocence
Of shames let fly against the sun
Paul, slobbering, rises from his chair
And plants his tongue upon that place.

White with contempt, the boy taunts him:
'Mad aunt! Crazed shepherdess! Fuck off!'
And knocks *Paul* down. *Paul* rises, feels
Inside the darkness of a pocket
A gun that yearns to reach its target,
Rimb's ice-black heart, the centre of
Their love turned hate: and aiming at
That centre, misses, wounds a finger.

The boy, become all child again,
Runs to his mother's womb – 'Police! Help!
Maman!' Two gendarmes rushing in
Take *Paul* away, to spend two years
Spieling poems – his penances!

   II PARIS 1873

Rimb rushes from the café, walks
With scything strides past fields hills towns
All day, and all night, sleepless, sees
Written across the dark his one
True poem true world of childhood, when,
At cock-crow, from his mother's house
He saw rainbows of dew cling on
Threads spiders wove between grass blades
Of meadows where hares raced with thudding
Reverberant hind legs that struck
The dawn's delirium like a drum,
While from low cottages small children
Ran out and pranced in jeering rings
Round steeples of their praying mothers.

*

Strode on and on till he reached Paris
That earliest hour when light and dark
Are ghosts laid in each other's arms,
Merged within one grey monochrome,
And the grey houses their own tombs –

When street cleaners come out to hose
Down avenues –
                            And in shirt sleeves
Waiters to tables set on pavements –
To throw out drunks in whose gross heads
Last night's brawls still reverberate –

When clattering shutters of shop windows
Rise upon bank clerks walking in
Circles of clocks that toll their lives –

III COMMUNE 1870

Beyond these *Rimb* saw his own ghost
Of two years past, the runaway –
1870, year of
Germany invading France –

Spike-helmeted jack-booted Prussians
Goose-stepping through French villages –

Yet at the centre Paris stood –
The flaming torch of all the free –
The Revolutionary Commune –

The People's Cause that called to him
Which, answering, he smuggled
His body through the Prussian lines

To Paris where, at a caserne
Of Communards, he brought that prize –
Freedom! his life to fight for theirs –
Freedom! – the workers' soldiers' sailors'

Deserters' pimps' whores' – such canaille
Shooting at sewage rats for food –

He brought them his rebellious youth
Which they received with jeers and blows
Obscenities and rape that pierced
His desecrated heart they spat
Out of their mouths with wads of chewed
Tobacco quids back to the gutter –

Back to his village and his mother.

IV VISIONARY

There, where he hid inside a barn
And cast his childhood from him, and
Cut himself off from all he knew,
His world from being human, 'Us',
But willed his 'I' be object 'IT'
On which the external history struck
Sounding below 'I' to ANOTHER
Deeper than conscious self which was
Visionary, Prophet, Magus of
One unreal final ultimate
Of Hell or Heaven, a new Love where
Poem knew poem as truth, as now
His poems knew *Paul*'s, as *Paul*'s knew his,
Poems that made love to poets, their makers.

V PARIS 1872

Paul to join whom he fled to Paris
Paul who received him as a god

And showed him off to drunk Parnassians
Took him to salons of Princesses –
Boy genius – wonder of a season –
Holy and damned – Saint Sebastian
And Satan – out of whose mouth streamed

351

Beauty and terror – all his world –
Impenetrable blazing diamond.

VI VIE LITTERAIRE

And yet some primal instinct in him
Of pagan slave or Gallic spunk
Detested them – the hostesses –
The inky scribes of feuilletons –

Also the poets – their scented beards –
Their agate eyes – their hearts laid bare –
Their childhoods weeping with dead mothers –
Their Testimonies and senile rhymes –

The paper-thin *vie littéraire*

And most of all he hated *Paul*
His cloying friend with heart that streamed
With blood for him the sneering boy –
And yet denied *Rimb*'s jeered demand
That *Paul* leave wife and babe for him.

          *

Rimb spat these from his mouth and strode
From Paris – whore of whores – to face
Past its Hell-gates, the modern world . . .

VII VOYAGES 1876–80

London – Milan – Stuttgart – Vienna –
On foot – trains – ships –

From Harderwijk on the Zuyder Zee
– Conscript of the Dutch colonial army –

On the *Prins van Oranje* –

– Skipped ship at Samarang –
Javanese jungles – natives –

Worked his way back

Bremen – Stockholm – Copenhagen –

Foreman of Mazeran-Viannay-Bardey –
Construction workers –
Cypriots – Greeks – Syrians –

   *

The sky a lottery from which
He drew his fiery ticket –
Africa! – Hurrah! – Harar!
Director of the Agence Pinchard.

   *

(Remains one photograph of *Rimb*
White-suited bristle-haired bronzed –

An explorer's eyes of ice that gaze
Past sacks of coffee-beans and heaps
Of animal-skins – and bottles –
Account books – ledgers –

Dreaming of mapping Zanzibar.)

VIII THE COMMUNIST MANIFESTO

O Capitalism
Imagination of the Real –
Captains of Industry,
Explorers, engineers, inventors –
Entrepreneurs,
Hearts of stone and brains of steel

History material on which
You chisel artefacts
– Canals
Incised through isthmuses –
Where two converging oceans kiss –

– And laying railways down
Across the continents – like arms
Of populations separated

Millennially till then
Embracing between mountain chains
On plains and valleys, their love beds.

  *

Also the gold stored in the banks.

IX CAPITALIST 1880–90

Rimb – capitalist –
Grown to full height with power to shape
The external world to match his will –

(Rejecting poetry's mirages)

Yet behind all
It is the dream that drives him on –
The dream that vows
It will come true.

  *

That after many journeyings
Of his crammed caravanserai
From weather-dented coasts – inland
Through deserts scattered with great stones
Locking within them memories
Of cities once raised on their columns –

To the interior of
The heart-shaped continent –

And after trading there with natives –
(Their scriptural black faces masks
Through which their bargaining eyes watched his) –

Bartering his medicine – beads – TRASH! –
With them for spices – ivory – gold –

After unending boredom of
Delays delays delays caused by
Bad faith – debts – credit to be raised
(Credit from Paris – hard to raise!) –

After infernal nights in rooms
Where stings of insects left in him
Fevers endemic to that zone –
His hard lithe body furrowed with
Trenches of premature old age –

After all these, he would return
Home to his village and his mother
And, standing on the threshold there,
Aged, lean, penitent, he'd watch
Where she sat stooped among her ruins –
Her stiff, starched pieties his fury
Was chariot over, linked with *Paul*'s:
Their ecstasy's excesses of
Red dreams released to violence by
Hashish and absinthe: journeys to
Cities the brothels of their wills.

*

But, to her, Africa was manifest
Insanity, his poems come true:
Continent of barbarian
Ebony natives, wielding spears,
Warring with naked tribes, their foes;
And, in the desert, gold-maned lions
Pouncing upon their prey – her son;
And in the jungle, serpents coiled,
Dropping from branches, on her son.

*

Then, entering her room, he would say:
'Mother, I am your son, returned –
No more the poet who made of words
Artefacts nothing but his dreams,
Shadows in light, mere fantasies –
Unreal vacuity.
                    Now I come,
Real magic valid in my hands,
Real wand of gold I gained, to change
Your poverty to riches, make
The palace dreamed come true. I am
The poem made solid that is real.'

X HOME 1886–91

3,500 francs in gold
Gunrunning from the coast –

Then suddenly there died
Proposed companions on that journey
Soleillet, Labatut.

And, against all warnings,
He went alone,
Travelling four months with
34 cameleers, threatening to strike,
30 camels, 2,000 rifles, 75,000 cartridges –

To the camp of Makonnen
Who called the guns 'out-dated'.

Then back to Harar
Where, from the mail awaiting him,
– Catalogues – treatises – bills –
A pamphlet falls – from Paris
A new review – *The Decadent* –
Fit organ of young poets –
An article by *Paul*, discovering

One genius, greatest poet of all,
Rimb –

who lets the pamphlet fall:

'DISGUSTING   PUERILE   OBSCENE!'

*

Writes home: 'Dear friends,
The cicatrice upon my thigh
Has made the whole limb gangrenous
And thick as all the body.
Having cashed all my savings
And had a litter made
(My own specifications!)
I have hired twenty bearers to
Carry me to the coast.'

*

The sun a red-hot piston rod
From the sky-centre
Pounding down on him – body and soul!
Days of fire and nights of ice
Circles of Hell
Moved through, that are God's Love,
Defied by him as he repeats
Childhood obscenities:
Cock cunt arse-hole etcetera
Spat back at Him.

*

Then at Marseilles, the hospital,
The death they all found beautiful –
Doctor – priest – mother – sister – all . . .

*   *   *

But, as he lay there, dying –
Remembering that cicatrice

357

Upon his thigh – (‘*my gilded*
Stamp of sin,’ to *Paul*)
Did he – too ill to speak – ask then:
‘Unto what God, of Heaven or Hell
– Spiritual or material –
Poetry or the Real –
Is this, my severed thigh,
Blood-sacrifice?’

Room

This room’s electric with those memories
Which, when he enters their invisible
Unanticipated zone, galvanize
His spirit to a shape his body had
Centuries, it seems, ago.
                                   Open the door –
The room’s ablaze with children
In their sloop made of two chairs
Where they play pirates.
                                   Points of fire, their hair,
Their eyes of ice, their laughter
The clashing swords of angels guarding Eden.
‘Come in!’ they shout, and mean to say ‘Get out!’

Then, standing at the window, seeing
Dusk absorb the green particulars
Of grass and trees, and make intenser
The glow of bricks and roses, he hears
Calling from the shrubbery, the voice
Of one long dead,
Poignant through the dark, that when she lived
He dared not answer.

Grandparents

Incredible to realize they've gone:
Matthew – Maro – their children – our grandchildren –
Saskia – Cosima – in the Renault
Festooned as for a wedding, with pink hands
Waving from windows blown farewells.
Matthew's parting smile above the wheel
Disappears down our lane – his face
Torn from a coloured postcard of our garden.
We go back to the house where Yesterday
Still scatters through the rooms the wreckage
Of cardboard boxes, toys, torn silver paper.
Our room that seemed to bulge with voices
And walls bounced off by Matthew's clarinet's
Billowing notes – relapsed to silence. We ourselves
Though ancient, not yet ghosts, feel two-dimensional
– Cardboard cut-outs of grandparents
With one soul, like some flower plucked at a picnic
A century ago – pressed between pages
Of an ancient tome – absorbing ink each side –
One chapter's ending and the next's beginning.
Well, do not let this silence – vacuum
Which, as they say, Nature abhors –
Be filled at any moment with our tears.

Black-and-White Photography

I

Brilliant lens, miraculous shutter – forceps –
Take up the object and translate it
Simplified to light and shadow –
The silent dead, the insolently living,
The kissed and kissing loved –
Translated now into the two-dimensional

Bright flowers of yesterday recorded, albumed in
The traveller's returning eye:
My fluted bride like a Greek column,
My daughter's face blurred by her breathing,
My diving friends before the war
Shot against waves that seem of marble.

II

I narrow my apertures to see objects in simple contrasts of
    black and white.
I dilate my lenses to light I need to produce an image not too
    faint nor too blurred.
I wear dark-glass filters to shade the boring public glare of the
    self-absorbed midday sun.
I select my angles enlarge my significant details and cut my
    irrelevant impressions from my frame.
I distort the most familiar details to totally new hideosities.
Sometimes I watch for hours in a dark square the lamps of
    cars trail ribbons through me.

III

Here are some photographs taken by Venus when she rose
    from the waves:
1) Sprouting breasts of San Marco looked down at from the
    air.
2) *In flagrante* spumings of gods and goddesses in striptease
    waters of a fountain in Rome.
3) Curves like whips in air on marble paving stones made by
    chariot wheels at Ephesus.
4) *Vaporetti* setting up the waves that eat away Venetian
    palaces.

IV

Ruin circling ruin circling ruin
And clattering round the toe stubs of antiquity

Tourists spilled from their cars and with their cameras
Clicking clichés of ghosts
Then clambering back and roaring to new graveyards.

v

The falling bomb photographs the fallen city
The rocket flaming into outer space
Photographs the dwindling Earth before
It lands on a dead star.

A First War Childhood

March 1916,
The middle of a war
– One night long
As all my life –
A child, I lay awake
On my bed under
The slant ceiling
Of the attic of The Bluff,
Our parents' house
On the Norfolk coast.

Beyond the garden
Rain-matted fields
Stretched to the edge
Of the cliff, below which
A roaring Nor'easter
Heaped up waves –
White-maned horses
Charging over rocks

(I thought: 'Deep down under sea
Submarines nose
Among shoals of fish
And waving seaweed

While high above
Zeppelins
Intent to bomb London
Throb through the night.
And near the cliff edge
Soldiers in a dugout
Keep watch on our lives.')

    Wrapped in my blanket
– A chrysalis
Wings not yet sprouted –
I stared up at
The ceiling skylight
Where, mile on mile,
Tons of dark weighed
Pressing on glass,
And stars like jewels
In cogs of a watch
Divided time
Into minutes and seconds.

    Out of that Nowhere
Surrounding all
So that any point anywhere
Was at the centre,
There fell a voice
Like a waterfall
Speaking through space

I AM   I AM   I AM

    Then a bomb exploded –
The night went up
In flame that shook
The shrubbery leaves,
And soldiers came
Out of dark speared with flame,
And carried us children

Into their dugout
Below the earth.

   Ear pressed against
The khaki uniform
Of mine, in his arms,
I could hear his heart beat –
With the blood of all England.

Worldsworth

Returned now, seventy years
Later, to the farmhouse
Beside the lake – finding
My way there as by instinct –
A sudden storm shuts down
The enormous view –
                              leaving
Only one drop of rain
Suspended from a leaf –

                    As through
The wrong end of a telescope
I look back to that day
Of August 1916
Our parents brought us here –
Because a Zeppelin,
Turned back from raiding London,
Damaged, across the coast,
Had jettisoned two bombs
Near Sheringham, our home.

   *

I see in glassy miniature
Each precise particular:

The van with us all in it
No sooner reaches the farmhouse
By Derwentwater than
We four children scramble out
To climb our first mountain:
CATBELLS its childish name –
With pelt of furze, fern, heather,
As tame for us to mount
As our donkey tethered by
The beach, at Sheringham.

     *

Against the skyline, Michael
With arms and legs an X
Yells he has reached the top . . .

     *

And all that summer was
Cornucopia that nature
Still pours profuse before me
Within my inmost eye
Like visions the old masters
Made frescoes of on walls:

Us rowing in our boat,
Us fishing, on the lake,
Us walking by the lake
Along the narrow road
A few feet from the water's
Rippling pellucid surface,
Distorting fish and weeds –

And on the road's far side
A ditch, and caves, where ferns
Unfurled heraldic tongues
Of glossy green which, under,
Concealed the dark brown spore.

But more than these I loved
The maidenhair fern with
Stalk fine as the coiled
Hairspring in my watch –
Its leaves minute green spots.

Then, from the road, a path
Led through a wood whose branches
Interweaving above
Seemed high as a cathedral
Sculpting out from shadow
Its own interior, within
Whose hush we stood, and watched
Under our feet the rain,
Dripping from that branched roof,
Collect into small puddles
On which huge black slugs drifted
Like barges on the Thames.

Beyond the wood, we came
Next to a clearing. Then
The rain stopped suddenly: the sky
Seemed one great sword of light
Raised above those bushes
Where berries, red and black,
Blazed like the crown jewels of
Some king much loved in legend
By his peace-loving people
(Among whom none were robbers),
Left on a hedge while he
Went hunting with his followers.

Beyond this there were fields
With slate walls between whose
Rough-hewn slabs, through shadows
Wedged between crevices,
Crystals like pinpoints pricked
Into the dark, their secrets.

But then the path traversed
The naked mountainside
Where, near it, lay the carcass
Of a dead ram, crawled over
By maggots, flies in swarms
As little caring whether
They battened upon eyes
Or guts or blood, as did
Those Zeppelins over London
Whether their bombs destroyed
Temples of stone, or flesh.

*

At dusk,
If there was no rain –
                              (great drops
Denting the flattened lake like boulders
Falling in molten lead,
Each one the centre of
Widening concentric circles) –

Our parents,
Seated in deck chairs on the lawn,
Read to each other poems

– The murmuring reached my bed –

Rhythms I knew called Wordsworth
Spreading through mountains, vales,
To fill, I thought, the world.

'*Worldsworth*', I thought, this peace
Of voices intermingling –
'Worldsworth', to me, a vow.

Six Variations

(Thoughts for Isaiah Berlin, arising from reading Pepys' Journal)

So busy: Pepys at Cambridge, 1660:

February 26: With my father –
Walked in the fields behind King's College
Chapel yard . . . Met Mr Fairbrother
Who took us both to Botolphe's Church
Where Mr Nicholas of Queens preached: text –
  'For thy commandments are broad.'

. . . Thence to dine with Mr Widdrington
Who had with him two fellow commoners
And a Fellow of the college, Mr Pepper . . .
Later, to Magdalen to obtain
The certificate of my brother's entrance –
After which Mr Pechell joined us
And we all sat in the Rose Tavern
Drinking the King's health until dark . . .
Back to our lodging next, then once more
To the Tavern again with Mr Blayton
And Mr Merle with a quart of wine.

I

Such talking drinking life – three hundred
And thirty years ago! Reading, I don't think:
Where are they now, those chatterers? – Thrust
In graveyards? Less than dust – salt sown
In ship-wrecked oceans? Blood-red rust
Of battlefields that crops
Green out of? Left, some relics
Rotting in attics – sword-hilt, snuff box,
Silver or ivory – skeletons
Cased in provincial museums?

II

No, when I read Pepys now, he and his cronies
Burn from their days and through my veins –
Their acts and passions one with those
Moving through mine! As though
To live meant to be tenant of
This temporary flesh through which
Continually the same life flows
Out of the past – through us, and to
Those generations yet unborn.

III

What do I speak but dead men's words?
What are my thoughts but dead men's minds?

IV

Well, there's the being conscious. *Now!*
Each separate life, an 'I' (a world,
To his own self) within which meet
All that's outside: the multitudes
That make this time – and the dead past
Buried within the present – and,
Light-years away, that furthest star
Proved, yet unseen; all pulsing through
My living flesh to make the future.

V

What haunts us now is not those ghosts
From the cased past, but from the future:
Ghosts of the unborn – aviators,
Powered with the means our times invented
To end all life on Earth, and leave
This planet a charred shell within

VI

The elemental Universe
Of minerals, fire, and ice,
Where are
Nor eyes to see nor ears to hear
The planets and the silences
The never-meeting distances
– Nor consciousness, nor Mind, wherein
The shaping atoms recognize
Their world within the words, the names
Met on the tongue, those points of flame.

The Alphabet Tree

(*To Valerie Eliot*)

Today when I woke
Soon as dawn broke
I saw a ladder
Set up against
The Alphabet Tree.

From on high a Voice spoke
'Today you must climb
Up the rungs of this ladder
Each one a letter
Of words in a poem
That you must write
Rhyme mirroring rhyme,
And complete by midnight
When, from A at the root,
Heaven-reaching, your head
Through the darkness will shoot
To strike letter Z.'

So I climbed up A, B,
C, D, E, F and G,
H, I, J and K
(I was almost halfway!)
And then L, M, N,
O, P, Q, R and S
(Seven more to success!)
U, V and W
(Bets on me double now!)
Until I was up
At the Tree's dizzy top.

So I struck letter Z!
Proud, I then read
The poem in my head.
But 'Alas!' the Voice said:
'Your poem is a flower
Whose petals will scatter
On the breeze in an hour,
Zeroed by Zephyr
And unwept by Zigeuner
Zizzing his zither
Or twanging guitar!

'But behold where on high
The entire ink-black sky
Is diamonded
With stars of great poets
Whose language unfetters
Every Alphabet's letters
Interweaving through Time
In rhythm and rhyme –
Where the living shall read
The more living – the dead!'

TWO POEMS (1995)

Timothy Corsellis

No gift this Christmas, Timothy Corsellis,
– Transport Transatlantic pilot –
Could equal this, your poem that reached me
Here, but with news that you were dead –
Shot down or lost mid-ocean . . . Drowned . . .

You write of that one time we met –
First and last meeting in a pub:
Outside, the Black-Out street with rubble
From last night's raid: within,
The stench and glamour – glass and brass –
Of the bar's proppers-up: grimaces,
Gesticulating in a mirror
Behind the barmaid's taps and bottles.
At tables in hushed corners, lovers
Whispering futures to each other.

Standing side by side together,
Out of that clamorous place, we hewed
A silence where the dead poets joined us
– Angel of Rilke, Keats's nightingale,
Spirits with us where we stood under
Shakespeare's white cliffs.
        Then we bade
Farewells outside. And you walked on
To join companions on the airfield:
Bill Sipprel, Michael Jones, Jim Mason –
Pilots, mind and purpose one –
Passionate wills identified
With wings and power of their machines:

Who flew into their deaths above
Us with the dead weight of our lives.

[1941/1995]

373

The Mythical Life and Love of D. H. Lawrence

D. H. Lawrence was a perfect little Oedipus
Loving his mother who loved him,
Hating his father, coal miner –
Who came back drunk each evening from the pit
And naked in the wash-tub in the parlour
Scrubbed coal-dust from his chest and thighs
Up which the black hair branched like ivy.

      Mother and son walked in the churchyard
Deep below which the father hewed
Black glistening minerals in a tunnel.
Happy, the two watched a Red Admiral
Flatten blackwhitescarlet wings
Trembling, against a tombstone. Then the boy ran
And, wrenching from the soil a pale anemone,
Chose her the starriest petal, saying:
'This for Eurydice, my bride,
From Orpheus, her lover-son,
To pledge his truth that when she dies
He'll follow her through Pluto's caverns
To the deep hollows of the Earth
And bring her back up to its surface.'

      When, ten years later, she lay dying
He travelled down the corridors
Of his own dying, to her cancer.
He threw himself beside her, weeping:
'Mother, whose body was the gateway
Through which I entered life, I go back
Now to that moment you and I
Were Word before we both were World,
To be rejoined in Death forever.'

      Just then a bird sang from the sunlight:
'Orpheus/Lorenzo, turn, look back at
Eurydice your mother/bride

Who wills your body as her corpse.'
Turning, he then looked back at her
And saw her eyes that searched for his
And felt her fingers clasping his
And heard her tears plead with him: 'Orpheus!
Follow me to this end, our death!'

Thrusting her from him then, he stamped
Her corpse down on the earth and ran
Out in the new day's sunlight.
                              'Glad!
Glad!' then that bird his sex sang. 'Follow
Me through the forest up the mountain
There, on the uttermost peak, awaken
Frieda/Brunnhilde locked in sleep
Bound down by chains of Intellect
Her husband/father Wotan wrought there!
Orpheus/Lorenzo, now be Siegfried,
Leap over palisades of fire
Awake Brunnhilde, clasp her to you
Flesh to your flesh, both resurrected
One soul one body in one love!'

Leaping the flames then, he embraced her,
There on the uttermost peak. The sun
Clanged in the sky with one wild note.
Their joy spired upward on their laughter –
Pinnacle whence they looked down at
His mother dwindled to her ghost.

They fled then to the Hochgebirge
Where, at an inn beside a lake
Watching the full moon gaze down on them
There, on a balcony, they made love.

'See how the moon among the stars
Mounts its O mirrored on the lake

As I do you,' he cried. 'Joined flesh
One with our spirits come full circle!'
      His body was her sword, her breasts
His roses when they woke to watch
The sun's renewing fingers pluck
The strung chords of the lute-shaped lake
Where fishermen drew in their nets
The quivering silver from the water,
Set upon the shore to dry.

      Their happiness was like a mirror
Hung in the corner of their room
Where, from their bed, they saw, reflected,
The summer limned in miniature:
The labourer in the vineyard, tending
The vines with arms upraised that bared
His chest all bronze; and in the cornfield
The reaper leaning on his scythe
With arrowing glance that pierced his girl
Sprawled on her back among the sheaves.

      But, in the distance, then they saw
Across the lake, a sad procession
Wind between cypresses, black flames,
Following an ox-drawn wagon where
A woman's corpse lay jolted from
The wooden wheels on the stone road.
Watching, his thoughts sprang to her: 'Mother!
Darling in Sunday best, black bonnet,
Black dress, black shoes, and beads all jet,
See, I can lift you up to look
Into this room. Here you will be
One with my marriage – join us here
Where all that we two, son and mother,
In the slum house between the slag heaps,
Looked at by lamplight in the parlour

Pictures of places far forever –
Have all come true – be with us here
Flesh of my flesh and flesh of Frieda
As Frieda, loving me, is yours.'

*

Last of those mourners, Frieda saw
Her children weeping for their mother.

She hated that he loved his mother.
He hated that she loved her children.

When she embraced him now she saw
His mother gazing through his eyes.

When he embraced her now, he felt
Her children leaping in her womb.

.

Dedicatees

T.A.R.H. Tony Hyndman
M.M.B. Muriel Buttinger (Gardiner)
Muriel Muriel Gardiner
Inez Inez Spender (Marie Agnes Pearn)
Natasha Natasha Spender (née Litvin)
H.S. Humphrey Spender
M.A.S. Michael Alfred Spender
W.H.A. W. H. Auden
W.J.S. William Jay Smith
W.G. William Goyen
F.C.C. Frances Cornford
V.W. Virginia Woolf
M.J. Michael Jones

Index of Titles and First Lines